I Believe…

I Believe…

The Catechism and You

Glen Argan

NOVALIS

I Believe . . .: The Catechism and You is published by Novalis Publishing.

© 1997 Glen Argan

Cover artwork: "Jesus walking on water," Lynn McIlride Evans
Cover design: Robert Vienneau
Layout: Gilles Lépine
Printed in Canada.

Novalis Editorial Offices
Saint Paul University
223 Main St.
Ottawa, Ontario
Canada
K1S 1C4

Novalis Business Offices
49 Front St. East, 2nd Floor
Toronto, Ontario
Canada
M5E 1B3

Canadian Cataloguing in Publication Data

Argan, Glen William, 1952–

    I believe– the catechism and you

Newspaper columns originally published in the Western

    Catholic reporter, 1995–1996.

ISBN 2-89088-851-7

    1. Catholic Church. Catechismus Ecclesiae
Catholicae. 2. Catholic Church–Catechisms.
I. Western Catholic reporter. II. Title.

BX1959.5.A74   1997   238'.2   C96–900972–0

NOVALIS

Contents

Preface

In late 1992, the Western Catholic Reporter, the newspaper of which I am the editor, conducted a readership survey. The most striking result from that survey was that our readers wanted to gain more understanding of the church's teachings on faith and morals from the newspaper. So we set about making changes to reflect that desire. To be sure, the changes were far from sweeping. But we did start using a syndicated series of articles which show how faith can come alive in daily living. And we added some new columnists and selected feature articles which responded to this desire.

By early December 1994, the *WCR* was planning another readership survey for later in the winter. One bitterly cold Saturday morning I drove to Lamont, a small town east of Edmonton, to address representatives from parishes in the region. I decided to try out the latest version of this readership survey as part of my presentation. The results from this group of about a dozen people were surprising. Again, there was a clear message — the *WCR* needs to do more to help readers understand what the church teaches about faith and morals.

Obviously, something more was needed than what we were doing. The hunger of Catholics to know about their church's teachings is strong and deeply felt. And we who work for the church have a responsibility to scour the shelves for food that will fill that hunger.

On my drive back to Edmonton on that sunny, freezing afternoon I resolved I would do something. The English translation of the *Catechism of the Catholic Church* had been released six months earlier. I decided to write a series of articles which would go through the *Catechism* section by section, sometimes explaining the content, sometimes reflecting on it.

The 50 articles on the first section of the *Catechism* which make up this book were published in the Western Catholic Reporter between April 1995 and June 1996. I am now well into writing the articles on the fourth part — Christian Prayer — and hope to complete the full series by June 1998.

I could have tried to cajole a theologian into writing these articles. Although I have a graduate degree in philosophy, I am a journalist, not an academic. But my sense is that our readers do not want an academic treatment of the faith. They want to know their faith so they can live it. Besides, I wanted to take on this challenge myself. I wanted to deepen my own faith, a goal which has been fulfilled more than I anticipated.

When the readership survey was conducted in the *WCR* in February 1995, the views of the general readership mirrored those of the small group in Lamont. Again, people overwhelmingly wanted the newspaper to teach more about faith and morals. In particular, dozens of people made pleas for the *WCR* to provide extensive material about the *Catechism*.

The series began with little fanfare but has developed a loyal and substantial following of readers. Many people have asked that these articles be grouped together in a book because they are finding the collection of *Catechism* articles which they have cut from the newspaper to be unwieldy. So this book is a response to that request as well as an attempt to find new friends for this collection of reflections. Those who have read the articles in the *WCR* will find the content of most to be largely unchanged. However, a couple have undergone major revisions thanks to reader criticisms and comments.

The biggest supporter of this project has been Edmonton Archbishop Joseph MacNeil. The archbishop has read all these articles prior to publication, made a few suggestions and given me loads of encouragement. At several events, he has urged the people of the archdiocese to read these articles.

My wife Nora Parker has also made important suggestions and, with our young daughters Natasha and Jennifer, has occasionally had to suffer with an absent-minded husband and Daddy pondering the meaning of some doctrine of the Catholic faith.

I also would like to thank Linda Noster, Warren Harbeck, Rev. Bruce Miles, Nicholas Jesson, many readers of the *WCR* and, of course, the Vegreville West Regional Pastoral Council, all of whom have goaded me or encouraged me or in some way contributed to this finished product.

Finally, I need to comment on the lack of inclusive language in the English translation of the *Catechism*. The decision to use non-inclusive language was an unfortunate one. For many, it is a barrier which prevents them from hearing the truths which the *Catechism* proclaims.

We have a Christian responsibility to be sensitive in how we speak. Language should promote understanding, not hinder it. The truths of the faith should be presented in a way which is perceived as speaking to all people. Failing to do so will only undermine the renewal which the *Cat-echism*'s authors hoped to inspire.

Nevertheless, while using the New Revised Standard Version as the basic text of the Bible, I have used the original English translation in quoting from the *Catechism*. I hope that readers will not find this too jarring in the few quotes which use non-inclusive language.

Edmonton
11 July 1996
Feast of St. Benedict

Introduction

Read: *Catechism of the Catholic Church*, nos. 1-25

The family Bible once held an honoured, but neglected, place in Catholic homes. It was important to have a Bible and to note the special times of passage — marriage, baptisms and First Communions — in the special section set aside for that purpose.

But in most homes, regular reading from that Bible did not occur. The Bible was something we had, not something we knew.

In the last 30 years, that has begun to change. Catholics have begun to blow the dust off the Bible, to read it, to study it and even to talk about it with other Catholics. This is one of the most remarkable changes to take place in the post-Vatican II church.

The publication of the English translation of the *Catechism of the Catholic Church* in mid-1994 threatens to launch yet another publication into the exclusive realm of treasured Catholic dust collectors. The *Catechism* is a weighty volume which needs to be digested in small morsels, rather than to be gulped down in a couple of readings. It was written as a reference book, not as a mystery novel. It uses prose which is at times difficult for the contemporary North American reader.

Moreover, its original intended audience was bishops, pastors and theologians. During the writing process, however, a shift occurred and the idea arose that the *Catechism* deserved a place in every Catholic home.

The publication of the *Catechism* represents a unique opportunity for the church — an opportunity to renew and deepen the faith of great masses of ordinary Catholics. But average lay Catholics will need help in wading through the 581 pages (not including indices) of the *Catechism*.

The opportunity: The *Catechism* states that "Periods of renewal in the church are also intense moments of catechesis" (#8). To study the faith with an open heart is to do more than acquire knowledge about some field of study. It is to engage in the renewal of the church and thus to contribute to the renewal of the world itself.

The obstacle: Many readers will need not so much an explanation of the content of the *Catechism* as a way of reflecting on that content. They are quite capable of reading the *Catechism*. But they may need encouragement to begin the task, stay with it and to reflect on the meaning of our faith.

My purpose in this book is to invite people to enter into each section of the *Catechism* and to explore, with an active mind, its spiritual treasures. This book only skims the surface of the *Catechism* which itself only provides an introduction to the great wealth of church teaching.

The *Catechism* needs feet. If it is to start walking in today's world, it needs to run up against the questions which we have as individuals and as a society. To this reflection on the *Catechism*, I have brought some of my own personal experiences. I have also tried to relate church teaching to prevalent attitudes and opinions in our culture. I do this because I believe the church's teaching has much to offer our confused, amoral and sometimes self-destructive society.

At the same time, I believe we are at a point where we need to reconstruct, or at least rediscover, the foundations of our faith. Since the Second Vatican Council, we have gone through an agonizing period of deconstruction. A once-stable Catholic culture has been shaken. In some ways, this has been good. The church was in need of and is receiving spiritual renewal.

But this period has also been catastrophic. Many, many people have lost their moorings and turned away from the faith. Dissension and contention over church teachings have been rampant. Discussion within the church has been notable more for its anger than for its charity.

This has perhaps been most evident on the liberal wing of the church. But "traditionalists" too have undermined the tradition by presenting it as a museum piece fixed in all its details at some unspecified point in the past. Vatican II has sometimes been presented as either unimportant or as a break with the tradition.

Tradition for Catholics, however, is a living, breathing tradition. The *Catechism* is faithful to the living tradition and draws more heavily on the documents of Vatican II than on those of any other church council. The *Catechism* serves not to guard a museum or to narrow our vision; it is an invitation to a wider and deeper faith. It provides a framework for conversations with each other and with our children about what is really meaningful in life.

I mention our children because of my sense that there is a growing generation gap in our church. Many of my elders were formed by the heady times of the 1960s. It led them to rebel against what they perceived as the stultifying pre-Vatican II church culture. They fought for greater openness and inclusiveness in the church.

2

But their grandchildren often see no need for rebellion. They have not experienced the pre-Vatican II church and are in no position to rebel against it. Sometimes, they have been raised in a way which is virtually normless. If they want to touch the ancient wisdom of the church, they have to find it for themselves because their elders have either forgotten it or are embarrassed by it.

Haunting me have been the words of the Franciscan spiritual writer Richard Rohr: "Our people are dying for lack of vision, for lack of transcendent meaning to name their soul and their struggles. . . . Why would a young person join a group of 50-year-old complainers who are unwilling to speak of God and joy and peace beyond comprehension?"

One would not immediately think of the *Catechism* as a joy-filled document. But it is a gateway to life in the Holy Spirit, whose fruits do include joy, peace, kindness and generosity. It is the basis of a vision which we must again offer the world, a vision which must not only reconstruct the church, but also contribute to the life of the world as we enter the third millennium.

That vision is the vision of Vatican II. It includes a deep respect for the accumulated wisdom of the body of Christ. It also includes a new emphasis on ecumenism, religious liberty and social justice. It is the fruit of a mature church, a church which knows who it is and is comfortable with itself. A church which is not afraid to learn from the world. A church which seeks to make its contribution to building a more just and human world.

Thanks in part to the leadership of an unusually gifted and holy pontiff, the church is coming out of its exile. And like the Jewish exiles who returned to Jerusalem, we must set out in hope to rebuild the city and the temple:

"You see the evil plight in which we stand: Jerusalem lies in ruins, its gates have been gutted by fire. Come, let us rebuild the wall of Jerusalem so that we may no longer be an object of derision! . . . They replied, 'Let us be up and building!' And they undertook the good work with vigour" (Nehemiah 2:17-18, *New American Bible*).

The *Catechism* is one part of that rebuilding task. My hope is that this little book will, through the intercession of Mary the Mother of God, be of some help in deepening the faith of its readers.

3

2

A Yearning for God

Read: *Catechism of the Catholic Church*, nos. 27-35

There was a time when I was far from God. Raised in a good Catholic family, I was nevertheless deluded by contemporary currents of thought. I came to see religion as a crutch, liturgy as empty ritual which offered no life and the church as a barrier to establishing a fully human society.

Born in the midst of the Baby Boom, I was a child of the 1960s. When John Lennon said the Beatles were more popular than Jesus, he seemed to me to be stating the obvious. They were certainly more popular with me than was Jesus.

What changed my mind and heart? Well, despite the barriers to faith in my life, I sensed the deep mystery inherent in all being. The world was too full of patterns and order for there not to be a Creator who cared deeply for humanity. And there was a powerful yearning in my heart, a yearning for something more and deeper than what I could feel and taste and touch.

I stumbled into reading and studying St. Augustine's *Confessions*. In the first paragraph, Augustine praised God and said, "You have made us for yourself and our heart is restless until it rests in you."

Those words haunted me and gave form to the yearning of my heart. I came to see that all human striving — for knowledge, for goodness, even for possessions — was rooted in a search for God. Does it make sense for us to spend our lives searching for God and for there to be no God? Surely not. At the very least, there needs to be some cosmic trickster who planted these yearnings in the human heart.

However, my own life experience and observations told me that, although the world has ample suffering and hardship, it is fundamentally a good place. I couldn't believe it was created by a trickster. The human soul, I concluded, can have its origin only in a being who has lovingly created this world in a way that calls forth the best that people are capable of.

And then I was led to a church community where it was apparent that worship need not be empty and boring. Worship could be full of both vigour and mystery. It could give life, rather than drain it. Through this community, I met people who had been animated by God's Spirit, whose lives were lived with meaning.

It became clear to me that religion was not a crutch, not a drug to get us through this miserable world so that we can have real fun after we die. Faith in God made it possible to live this life in a better way. Instead of giving people an escape from this world, it enables us to be transformed and to transform this world.

The *Catechism of the Catholic Church* validates the way I came to know God. It suggests that people do not need a blinding inspiration or a direct experience of God to believe in him. We can discern God's existence through the world — through such realities as order and beauty.

We can also discover God through the human person — through "his openness to truth and beauty, his sense of moral goodness, his freedom and the voice of his conscience, with his longings for the infinite and for happiness" (no. 33). The *Catechism* quotes the Second Vatican Council which describes the human soul as the "seed of eternity we bear in ourselves, irreducible to the merely material."

Reason and experience can provide a gateway to God. They do not, however, take us to him through strict logical necessity. Many people reject God. Many others, through no apparent fault of their own, fail to recognize God. For Christians, the existence of unbelief is disconcerting. It represents both a puzzling theological challenge and a reality to help people overcome.

3

The Mystery of Unbelief

Read: *Catechism of the Catholic Church*, no. 37

One issue Christians must face is why some people do not believe in God.

Central to our way of thinking is that Jesus came to bring salvation to everyone and that there is a restlessness in each person's heart which can only be stilled through an intimate relationship with God.

If this is so, why do some people hear God's word and refuse to believe?

The simple answer is freedom. God doesn't force himself on anyone. If there were no possibility of unbelief then being a believer would have no merit. We are not called to be God's robots, but rather to be cooperators with God. And we all fail to cooperate to a greater or lesser extent.

When I look back at the years I strayed from the church, I see a number of reasons. As I became a teenager asserting my own autonomy, I rebelled against the things I formerly took for granted. I fell prey to worldly ideologies and my own sinfulness. I vainly believed that I knew more than the church which I came to see as a source of repression.

To be sure, identifiable Catholics were not always great witnesses to the transforming power of God. (Now, of course, people can say that about me!)

Pope Pius XII briefly described how we can find the Gospel difficult and demanding and thus deceive ourselves into believing that it is false or doubtful (see *Catechism*, no. 37). However, I don't know if I found the Gospel difficult in my teenage years. If someone had made me aware of how difficult it is, I might well have been more attracted to it. For, if nothing else, I was a youthful idealist in search of a cause to commit my life to.

In his book, *Crossing the Threshold of Hope,* Pope John Paul confronts the problem of the existence of unbelief. The pope is asked, "If God exists, why is he hiding?"

The pope's response is provocative, challenging to the non-believer. While agreeing that we do not yet see God face-to-face, the pope says, "it seems that he has gone as far as possible (in revealing himself). In a certain sense, God has gone too far!"

The problem is with us, the pope suggests. We are unable "to tolerate such closeness." By revealing himself in the person of Jesus Christ, God is to an extent "obscure" to us, "because man is not capable of withstanding an excess of mystery" (pp. 37-41).

The New Testament is rife with examples of Jesus and angels saying "Be not afraid!" A human reaction to the presence of the divine is fear. But the best human response to the divine is to face down the fear and accept the loving presence of God.

That's easier to say than to do, however. The fear of taking that first step towards God is a common experience among converts. Once one has crossed the threshold, one wonders why one was afraid. But, before the crossing is made, there can be a time of genuine terror. We stand at the brink and we must make a choice which has fundamental importance for our lives.

The existence of unbelievers is a sign that this is a real choice, not a sham. But, if we choose to cooperate with the God who draws close to us, we will open ourselves to a fullness of life which we didn't know was possible.

4

Our Limited Knowledge of God

Read: *Catechism of the Catholic Church*, nos. 39-53

With all this mystery, can we talk meaningfully about God? Words cannot capture that which is beyond all words. Perhaps we should take the advice of Ludwig Wittgenstein who proclaimed, "What we cannot speak about we must pass over in silence" (*Tractatus Logico-Philosophicus,* 7).

Wittgenstein, a leading twentieth-century secular philosopher, treated philosophy as a ladder which leads us to higher awareness. But once one has climbed the ladder, that person must throw it away and "see the world aright."

To a point, Wittgenstein is correct. Our knowledge of that which is beyond speech is strictly limited. St. Thomas Aquinas wrote that we cannot grasp what God is, only what God is not. And the Fourth Lateran Council stated that, although there are similarities between God and creatures, the dissimilarities are infinitely greater.

Still, if this were the end of it, humanity would be in deep trouble. The best one could hope for would be mystical intuitions of "the inexpressible, the incomprehensible, the invisible, the ungraspable." But we could not pass on those intuitions to anyone else. We would be left with private "knowledge," not real knowledge because it could not be transmitted to others.

The *Catechism* and Scriptures would be idle babbling, of little use to anyone who wants to know God. If we take them seriously, we would be engaging in idolatry. Are Scripture and church teaching just a ladder we must toss away once we reach the top?

More than human pondering and reasoning is needed to reach a sure knowledge of God. Reflection on God's creation and human reasoning can make us aware God exists. But for us to know God and to enter into a relationship with him, something else must occur. God must reveal himself to us.

In fact, God has done that by offering a covenant to his people. Through the covenant, he gives us his love. And God has revealed himself most fully through his incarnation in the person of Jesus Christ. We can know God because God has chosen to show himself to us.

We can find God by seeking him. Through natural reasoning and reflection we can become aware of the ineffable holiness of That Which Is Totally Other. But there is a surer and fuller way of coming to know God — by allowing him to come to us.

God can enter my heart through his inspired word in Scripture. He can transform my life through Baptism and Confession. He can enter my body through the Eucharist.

Through Jesus Christ and his church, God has given us a path to knowing him which we could never find on our own. History is rife with examples of people who gained a glimpse of God but who fell into idolatry or despair either because they were unaware of God's revelation or because they turned their backs on it.

Even the great philosopher Wittgenstein saw his insights turned into a golden calf. After publishing his *Tractatus* in 1919, he retired from philosophy. But then a school of philosophy grew up, supposedly rooted in his thinking, but which turned science into a god. Convinced these philosophers misunderstood the thrust of what he was saying, Wittgenstein came out of retirement to set things straight.

But, as far as we know, Wittgenstein never came to an act of faith — he never came to see that we don't have to climb a ladder to That Which Is Beyond Speech, that God has come down to us. He never realized that the Bible and the church are not ladders to be tossed away after they have been climbed, they are a constant and sure guide to the truth which comes from God.

On our own devices, we cannot stand face to face with Jesus, saying with Peter, "You are the Messiah, the Son of the living God." Nor will we hear Jesus respond, "Flesh and blood has not revealed this to you, but my Father in heaven" (Matthew 16:16-17).

Few of us are as intellectually gifted or as devoted to spiritual seeking as was Wittgenstein. But, if we have faith, we have something much greater than a lonely spiritual quest. We have received God's gift to us, the fullness of revealed truth.

5

Covenant with God

Read: *Catechism of the Catholic Church*, nos. 54-73

In one of his whimsical novels, the American author Kurt Vonnegut speaks of the Utterly Indifferent God. This God creates humanity and then walks away, leaving us to our own devices.

Vonnegut leaves us with a despairing picture of the human condition. It is worth noting that Vonnegut's outlook was shaped by his experiences as a prisoner of war held in Dresden, Germany. He saw the unspeakable horrors which befell that city when the Allied Forces fire-bombed it in 1945.

The future novelist perhaps asked himself how a loving God could allow such devastation and suffering to occur. To Vonnegut, we need to say that the horrors he witnessed were the work of humanity, not of God. The puzzle for the Christian believer is why God remains faithful to us in the face of our repeated and abominable sins.

The answer given by the Jewish and Christian Scriptures is that God, far from being indifferent, has freely bound himself to his people in a covenant relationship. He will love us and be gracious to us, no matter what we do.

When the first humans fell into sin, God washed them away in a great flood. He saved only Noah and his clan and started anew. But this time, God made a covenant with all creation, promising never again to bring down such destruction. He would be faithful no matter how much we turned away from him.

This unconditional love is the hallmark of the covenant. In a contract, one is bound only to the extent that the other party fulfills their end of the deal. Once that party has violated the pact, the other is freed from his or her obligations. A contract protects two parties from abuse by each other. But a covenant is a promise, not a form of protection.

The most common human experience of a covenant is the marital bond between a man and a woman. Marriages inevitably break down when they are seen as contracts in which one party need only uphold their end of the bargain to the extent that the other party does. Marriage is rooted in forgiveness, in throwing the other's sins into the sea of forgetfulness. Marriage needs more than justice, it needs mercy.

Again and again, the Old Testament compares God's relationship to his people with that of a bridegroom to his bride. One of the most poignant testimonies in the Hebrew Scriptures is that of Hosea, the man who remains faithful even though his wife deserts him. Hosea's love is a symbol of God's love. That love remains steadfast and punishes the unfaithful one only in order to bring her back. Eventually, that goal is accomplished.

This is not an indifferent God; it is a God who suffers and weeps because of the unfaithfulness of his people. Never does he turn his back on them as they do to him.

Moreover, God promises that he will show us a way out of our constant infidelity. "The prophets proclaim a radical redemption of the people of God, purification from all their infidelities, a salvation which will include all the nations" (*Catechism*, 64).

This salvation takes place through a person, Jesus Christ. In and through Christ, God shows us, in as complete a way as is possible, that he is close to us. God shares all the trials of our humanity — he accepts abuse and a horrible death. And he does this while being deserted by his closest friends and followers.

Is this the action of an Utterly Indifferent God?

It is not possible for God to be in any greater solidarity with us than he was in the person of Jesus Christ. God smashes the hold that sin has on our lives. He also gives us the ultimate example of how to live.

The new covenant which God offers through Christ's death and resurrection is the most God can offer us. It reveals everything. It contains everything. There is no point in looking for some meaning beyond Jesus because there is nothing more to be found. To be fulfilled, we need only accept the share in divine life which Jesus offers us through baptism and to live out that baptism by walking in Jesus' footsteps.

This is the covenant God offers us. What will be our response?

6

The Living Tradition

Read: *Catechism of the Catholic Church*, nos. 74-95

Scott Hahn, today a professor at a Catholic university in Ohio, was once a fervent anti-Catholic, schooled in the beliefs of Protestant fundamentalism. Hahn was led to the Catholic Church, at least in the early stages, by a process of intellectual conversion.

One day, a student asked him where in the Bible it states that faith is rooted in Scripture alone — a key tenet of the Reformation. "I said what any professor would say, 'What a dumb question!'" he recalled.

But the question haunted him. If the entire content of the faith is specified by Scripture, why doesn't the Bible tell us that?

Hahn began asking leading Protestant theologians the question. They too brushed it off as dumb.

But he found, rather than teaching that Scripture alone is the basis of faith, St. Paul urged Christians to "hold fast to the traditions that you were taught by us, either by word of mouth or by our letter" (2 Thessalonians 2:15). Right there, Paul was teaching that there is more than Scripture, that there is an oral tradition of faith.

And, in another place, Paul calls the church "the pillar and bulwark of the truth" (1 Timothy 3:15).

Working purely on the basis of his own literal fundamentalism, Hahn found that it takes more than the literal word of Scripture to root a Christian faith. That more is the church, the living tradition of faith, handed down from the apostles and reflected on by the body of believers over the centuries.

This is a crucial understanding to arrive at in our society which is rapidly losing its collective memory. We are becoming ruled by a tyranny of the present which ultimately says that anything beyond the present sensation is nostalgia.

But the human person is much more than a passive receiver of sensations. God has given us the ability to interpret, reason and judge. Our memories as individuals and our memory as a church and a society come about by our using those abilities. And our memory can hold forth a vision of a world different than the one in which we live in the here and now. Moreover, there is no memory that has not gone through some interpretation.

The *Catechism* is an introduction to the collective memory of the church. The content of faith is not simply a piece of data given to us. It is something, rooted in Scripture, mulled over by God's people, further conclusions drawn by church councils, and received and re-integrated by God's people today.

Faith is a process of interpretation. Just like our personal memories, such interpretation is rooted in reality — Scripture and definitive church statements. Some memories are true and others are fabrications. But our stories become richer by being re-told and re-interpreted. And we have what the Second Vatican Council called "the living magisterium of the church" to guide God's people towards interpretations which are reliable.

Unlike what Protestant fundamentalists think, this development of church tradition does not add anything to the faith which Jesus gave to the apostles. That would be a vain and foolish thing to attempt. But the church's reflection does deepen and make present for our own age and our own lives what Jesus taught to the apostles.

Scott Hahn used his own mind, asked questions and ultimately rebelled against the act of turning Scripture into an idol. He came to see that the Bible is the living word of God which bears fruit as people relate it to their own lives.

Just as Hahn's faith would have been cheated if he had not asked and held fast to his questions, so the faith of our church will be cheated if we do not ask questions and fervently seek out answers to them.

We need to be faithful and obedient to God's word and the church's tradition, but we also need to question. It is by holding fast to our questions that we will help to deepen the church's tradition for the generations to come.

(For more about Hahn's journey of faith, read *Rome Sweet Home: Our Journey to Catholicism* by Scott and Kimberly Hahn, Ignatius Press, 1993.)

7

The Fullness of Scripture

Read: *Catechism of the Catholic Church*, nos. 101-133

One of the driving forces behind the Protestant Reformation was the desire to make the spiritual power of Scripture available to all God's children. This goal was, and remains, an honorable one.

But all good things, pushed too far, can have catastrophic results. In this case, not only did the reformers want to take the padlock off the Bible, but some asserted that it was through Scripture alone, unimpeded by human interpretations, that Christians could come to true faith. Such faith would be purified, freed of the accretions of 1,500 years, and would sparkle in the sun as did the early faith of the apostles.

Of course, as the reformers read the Scripture, they developed an understanding of it. Human understanding — for good or for ill — is always rooted in interpretation. Over the centuries, this freeing of Scripture inevitably led to new sets of tradition — tradition different from that of the Roman Catholic Church, but tradition nevertheless.

The twentieth century has seen a further development — biblical literalism. Upset that Protestantism was also developing a constantly refined body of interpretations of Scripture, fundamentalists sought to return permanently to a non-interpretive state of direct acceptance of the word of God. It didn't work. Now, there are thousands of Protestant denominations and non-denominational churches, each with their own understanding of the Bible.

The Roman Catholic tradition is rooted in the belief that a full understanding of Scripture is impossible outside the tradition. Scripture itself is interpretive — it includes some things and leaves out many.

John concludes his Gospel by admitting that he has interpreted Jesus' life: "There are also many other things that Jesus did: if every one of them were written down, I suppose that the world itself could not contain the books that would be written" (21:25). John chose which aspects of Jesus' life to include in his Gospel based on what he believed the Christian community of his day needed to know.

Moreover, the church spent centuries discussing which writings were divinely inspired before it decided which would be included in the Bible. Once the canon of Scripture had been determined, learned writers continued combatting errors of interpretation. This period of the early church fathers began the process of developing church doctrine in opposition to faulty interpretations — heresies — which arose. But it was the church which unearthed and defined the meaning inherent in Scripture. Scripture does not stand alone.

To restrict our reading of Scripture to its literal sense is to cheat ourselves of the full spiritual wealth contained in the holy books. The *Catechism of the Catholic Church* distinguishes three senses beyond the literal in which we can and ought to read Scripture in order to grasp the fullness of its message (see nos. 116-117).

For example, we can read the story of Moses leading the people out of Egypt as an historical account. But the early church fathers wrote that the story should not be left at that level. We ought to see the Old Testament as containing "prefigurations of what (God) accomplished in the fullness of time in the person of his incarnate Son" (*Catechism*, 128).

One of the earliest fathers, Tertullian, wrote that, "When the people, willingly leaving Egypt, escaped from the power of the King of Egypt by passing across the water, the water destroyed the king and all his army. What could be a clearer figure of baptism? The peoples are delivered from the world, and this is done by the water, and the devil, who has hitherto tyrannized over them, they leave behind, destroyed in the water."

Tertullian's account of the exodus is highly interpretive. But its interpretation leads us to a deeper understanding both of the exodus and of baptism.

The French Jesuit, Jean Danielou, showed how the early church fathers constantly used the Old Testament to unpack the meaning of the New. His conclusion: "The deeds of Christ are charged with biblical memories which tell us the true significance of these deeds" (*The Bible and the Liturgy,* p. 7). The *Catechism* makes the same point: "The New Testament lies hidden in the Old and the Old Testament is unveiled in the New" (no. 129).

In short, we cheat ourselves of the vast wealth of spiritual resources in the Bible if we try to limit it to its literal meaning.

The Catholic doctrinal tradition unearths that wealth from beneath the literal meaning of Scripture. To be sure, this task of unearthing is a perilous one, one which has many potential pitfalls. That is why we need the sure guidance of the church's magisterium to guarantee that our reading of the Bible is not a mere projection of our own biases onto the Scriptural text.

One more thing needs to be said. Fundamentalists read the Bible and read it often. We can hardly hope to go deeper than they do in our understanding unless we too read Scripture regularly. We cannot have access to biblical treasures unless we dig for them.

8

The Obedience of Faith

Read: *Catechism of the Catholic Church*, nos. 142-165

"By faith, man completely submits his intellect and his will to God."

        – Catechism, no. 243

When I hit my mid-teens, I decided that I was too good for the church. I felt that I had a strong spiritual life — not that I did much to develop it — and that the church was more a hindrance than a help to my reaching God.

All those rules and rituals were fine for children. But I was mature now and such things were only an impediment to my relationship with God. I was intelligent, a free thinker and could meet God in my own way. The notion that I should actually obey anyone or anything was an anathema.

Oh, the arrogance of it all! Nearly 2,000 years of Christian history had preceded me and I had next to nothing to learn from it. Jesus became physically present in the Eucharist, but somehow I thought I could, on my own, develop an even greater intimacy with God.

Somehow, I never stopped to think that I was but a creature and God, the Creator. My very being and the being of all things was due to a decision by God. Who was I to put myself above the church and on a par with God in my own private spirituality?

One could not dignify this spirituality by calling it faith. For faith means not only a belief in things unseen, but also submission to a power greater than oneself. Submission in every aspect of one's being.

We don't think this way in Western society. We don't see ourselves as stewards of creation, but as masters of all. We will not submit to anything, because it could impose limits on us. Better to hang loose, play cool and not take any stands which could lead to commitments. There is no more frightening word in our individualistic culture than "obey."

But John Cougar Mellencamp sings, "You'd better stand for something or you're gonna fall for anything." Likewise, G. K. Chesterton said a lack of faith doesn't mean you believe nothing, it means you'll believe anything. And the prophet Isaiah wrote, "If you do not stand firm in faith, you shall not stand at all" (7:9).

People may not have faith in God, but they act as though they believe they can find lasting happiness with a 4,500-square-foot house or by performing rituals with crystals.

The most basic stance a person can make against such idolatry is to be baptized. To be baptized is to allow one's life to be taken over by Christ. Commit yourself to living out that baptism and you'll fall for nothing. Except that you'll have fallen totally in love with Jesus Christ. You'll obey his commandments and go where he sends you.

Years after renewing my Christian commitment, the scariest words in the Gospel were those Jesus spoke to Peter after the resurrection: "When you grow old, you will stretch out your hands and someone else will fasten a belt around you and take you where you do not wish to go" (John 21:18).

The fear those words held for me pointed to my need for further conversion. The only people who would accept going to a place where they don't wish to go are those who trust the Lord totally. Who has such trust?

The *Catechism of the Catholic Church* holds up Abraham as "the model of such obedience" and Mary, the Mother of God, as "its most perfect embodiment" (no. 144). Indeed, through Abraham and Mary, we see that obedience to God does not diminish our humanity, but rather makes it fruitful. Through the death of our own schemes and plans of action, we find life beyond anything one might imagine. In Abraham, such life meant descendants more numerous than the stars in the sky; in Mary, a church which makes Christ's body physically present in the world today. All that from saying, "Be it done to me according to your word."

Real maturity comes from being like a child, from learning to obey. If God created us, our fulfilment comes from doing his will. It is by bowing that we stand. It is by dying that we can have life.

9

The Chain of Believers

Read: *Catechism of the Catholic Church*, nos. 166-184

"No one can have God as Father who does not have the church as mother."
— St. Cyprian, quoted in the *Catechism*, no. 181

Since the Second Vatican Council, the Catholic Church has been deeply blessed by the growth in millions of people of a sense of having a personal relationship with Jesus Christ.

This development is overwhelmingly positive. It moves faith beyond simply showing up for religious rituals to a dynamic growing force in each person which can bring the news about Jesus into the lives of many others.

The pitfall in this development is that it can sometimes lead to an individualistic faith — a faith so focused on the relationship between Jesus and me that the church and the rest of the world are forgotten. Ultimately, we may have to ask whether a purely Jesus-and-me relationship is faith or if it is narcissism.

St. Cyprian and other church fathers are clear about this. It is in the church, in the community of believers, that our faith is made real. The *Catechism of the Catholic Church* reminds us, "You have not given yourself faith as you have not given yourself life" (no. 166). And later: "Because we receive the life of faith through the church, she is our mother" (no. 169).

The seeds of my own faith were planted and nurtured by my parents who were convinced that faith in God is the most important aspect of a person's life. My faith grew in the Catholic school and parish I attended as a child through the witness of teachers, priests and my peers. After lying fallow for a few years, it was reinvigorated during my two years teaching at Campion College of the University of Regina by the personal witness of faculty members and by the dynamic worship community at that college.

My faith has been supported by numerous groups I've been involved in and conferences I've attended. It also has grown through contact with difficult people, people who have seemed to present roadblocks, but who were really opening new doors. And now it is fed by the powerful witness of my wife and the joy-filled spirits and everyday demands of my children.

But even if I had none of this, even if I only had the Bible to build my faith on, the church would still be my spiritual mother. For God did not hand down the Bible, carved on stone tablets. The books of the Bible contain the inspired word of God, but it took the people of Israel and the leaders of the Christian church centuries to decide which works were divinely inspired and ought to be included in the Bible and which ought to be left out. The Bible is both a divine and a human creation.

Jean-Paul Sartre, the atheist philosopher, wrote that "hell is other people." For Christians, the way to heaven is with other people. We can see the footsteps of the Holy Spirit throughout our lives, but the Holy Spirit most often acts through the free choices of other people. Only rarely, does the Spirit act directly. To say that faith is only between me and Jesus is to be blind to the places where God is perhaps most active.

Thomas Merton, the Trappist monk who lived most of his last years as a hermit, once described a mystical experience of oneness with secular humanity:

"In Louisville, at the corner of Fourth and Walnut, in the centre of the shopping district, I was suddenly overwhelmed with the realization that I loved all those people, that they were mine and I theirs, that we could not be alien to one another even though we were total strangers.

"It was like waking from a dream of separateness, of spurious self-isolation in a special world, the world of renunciation and supposed holiness. The whole illusion of a separate holy existence is a dream" (*Conjectures of a Guilty Bystander,* p. 156).

Holiness is not self-isolation, it is oneness with and love for humanity. There is no separate holy existence. There is the body of Christ which has fed us and which we must feed in return. "Our love for Jesus and for our neighbour impels us to speak to others about our faith. Each believer is thus a link in the great chain of believers" (*Catechism,* no. 166).

A Prayer Which Transforms Us

Read: *Catechism of the Catholic Church*, nos. 185-197

This is an odd sort of prayer, the Apostles' Creed. It doesn't praise or give thanks to God. Nor does it ask for anything, not even forgiveness.

The Creed doesn't do the sorts of things we normally expect a prayer to do. Rather, it simply seems to asserts that a list of propositions is true. What sort of prayer is that?

Yet, the Creed is one of two prayers at the centre of the *Catechism of the Catholic Church*. The other is the Lord's Prayer, the Our Father.

Together, exposition of the content of these two prayers makes up close to half of the church's chief reference book on the faith.

Moreover, the *Catechism* puts great stock in the recitation of the Creed. "To say the Creed with faith is to enter into communion with God, Father, Son and Holy Spirit and also with the whole church" (no. 197).

Now, reciting a list of propositions is not what we normally think of when we recall instances of communion with God. When we think of such moments, many of us tend to think of experiences such as watching the sun rise over the Prairie horizon. When we think of communion with others, we might think of great conversation, aided by a few beers, with close friends around a campfire.

Reciting propositions pales in comparison with such experiences of oneness with God, nature and humanity.

The late British writer C. S. Lewis recalled giving a talk on Christianity to a group in the air force. An old hard-bitten officer got up and told him, " 'I've no use for all that stuff. But, mind you, I'm a religious man too. I know there's a God. I've felt him: out alone in the desert at night: the tremendous mystery. And that's just why I don't believe all your neat little dogmas and formulas about him. To anyone who's met the real thing they all seem so petty and pedantic and unreal.' "

Lewis admitted the man "probably had a real experience of God in the desert. And when he turned from that experience to the Christian creeds, I think he really was turning from something real to something less real."

He compares the man's experience in the desert with sailing the ocean. Looking at a map of the ocean is far less real than sailing on it. But the map, he notes, "is based on what hundreds and thousands of people have found out by sailing the real Atlantic. . . . (And) if you want to go anywhere, the map is absolutely necessary."

His conclusion: "Doctrines are not God: they are only a kind of map." What the man experienced in the desert "was certainly exciting, but nothing comes of it. It leads nowhere. . . . That is why a vague religion — all about feeling God in nature and so on — is so attractive. It is all thrills and no work" (*Mere Christianity*, pp. 131-32).

Lewis gives us a start in understanding the nature of the Creed. But when you get down to it, the Creed is more like a wedding vow than like a map. To call it a list of propositions does not do justice to the Creed. Maps and propositions aim to describe a reality outside of oneself. But while the Creed does that, it also makes a statement about the basic orientation of one's life.

The Creed does not begin "It is true that . . .". Rather, it begins with "I believe . . .". Thus, it describes both an objective and a subjective reality.

In marriage, we promise to live in a certain way, a way quite different than how we lived previously. The wedding vow makes a promise, rather than a prediction, about the future. Now, the vow is not the experience of communion which gave rise to these two people committing themselves to each other. But it is a promise to make a lasting communion — a communion of much greater importance than a mystical moment in the desert.

Baptism is our wedding with God and his people. It is a radical reorientation of our lives. No longer will our main focus in life be on what is visible and practical. We are now turned towards the invisible. We live in the visible world as pilgrims from another kingdom, pilgrims who will influence the visible world with the values of the invisible. Together, we Christians are wedded to the unseen God who became flesh in the person of Jesus Christ and who continues to be present among us today.

So, if the Creed presents us with doctrine — 12 articles of faith — that doctrine must always be at the service of spirituality — our drawing close to this God. This is a point particularly well appreciated in the Christian East.

Says Russian Orthodox Father George Florovsky: "The church gives us not a system, but a key; not a plan of God's city, but the means of entering it.

"Perhaps someone will lose his way because he has no plan. But all that he will see, he will see without a mediator, he will see it directly, it will be real for him; while he who has studied only the plan risks remaining outside and not really finding anything."

The Orthodox tend to resist the dogmatic formulations of the Christian West. Such resistance stems not from disagreement with the articles of faith, but from a fear of over-emphasizing the map and ignoring the spiritual communion between the individual and God.

The Roman tradition has a response. It can point to the multitude of evils in the contemporary world and maintain that evil runs rampant because society has cast aside all maps. A subjective communion not anchored in objective truth can run aground on the rock of relativism.

We need not choose between doctrine and spiritual communion. We need to choose both. We need to reorient our lives toward the invisible God. The Creed, like a wedding vow, is an essential step in that reorientation. But we do not carry out the reorientation by reciting these words; we do it through the decisions and actions of daily life.

11

The Name of God

Read: *Catechism of the Catholic Church*, nos. 198-221

The story of God speaking to Moses from the burning bush (Exodus 3-4) is one of the most striking stories in the Bible. Reading that story, it is almost impossible not to be struck by the wonder of it. We go about our lives, as surely Moses did, doing an honest day's work and trying to help our families and friends. Extraordinary events are few and far between.

So when one hears a story of a bush which burns without being destroyed and the voice of God emerging from that bush, one immediately becomes caught up in the miraculous nature of that event.

But tucked away in that amazing occurrence is another event which radically altered the way a primitive people understood God. These nomadic people would have understood God as present in nature and the manifestations of God as inextricably linked to the place where they occurred. If one had a mystical experience by a maple tree, for example, then that tree would forever be seen as imbued with magical power.

There was little sense that God could be beyond space, that God could be something greater than that tree itself. So, each tribe had its own gods, each tied to a particular place or object.

It is in this context that Moses, after receiving his call to liberate the Hebrew people, asks a question which strikes us as odd, but which would have been essential for someone of his understanding. Moses asks God his name. When Moses tells the people God has sent him, they will naturally wish to know which god this is.

God's reply is enigmatic. "God said to Moses, 'I AM WHO I AM.' He said further, 'Thus you shall say to the Israelites, "I AM has sent me to you"'" (Exodus 3:13-14). God does not give himself what we would call a proper name. He does not say, "My name is Fred." But neither does he say, "I am the God beyond all knowing, the God beyond all names."

With his name, Yahweh God establishes his closeness to his people. As the *Catechism* puts it: "God has a name; he is not an anonymous force" (no. 203). Because God has a name, we can establish a personal relationship with God. We can call on God; we can invoke his name.

But Yahweh God is not a God trapped by space and time. We cannot simply identify this God with the burning bush. His name points us toward mystery, to something far beyond our ability to comprehend. This is not simply one God among other gods, but an eternal God, the God who is the seed and the root of all being. God may be manifest in nature, but God is beyond the natural realm.

This has enormous implications for how we ought to live our lives. God is close to us, very close, but also far greater than us. We can establish a relationship with God. But we cannot control him by speaking his name or offering him sacrifices. "Faced with God's fascinating and mysterious presence, man discovers his own insignificance" (*Catechism*, no. 208). People are subject to God and not God to us.

This combination of God's transcendence and God's closeness is exceedingly difficult for us to hold together. The Jewish leaders at the time of Jesus waited for a messiah. But they could not accept that God would take human form. When Jesus identified himself with God, they tore their garments and had him put to death.

Peter did accept that Jesus was God, but thought that Jesus' divinity was a ticket to glory in this world. When it became clear that Jesus was to be put to death, Peter proclaimed, "I do not know this man." He could not accept how much like us God would become.

Pope John Paul describes the development of the synagogue and of Islam as protests against Christianity's insistence that God loves us so much that he would die to redeem us from our sins.

The pope writes: "Neither can accept a God who is so human. 'It is not suitable to speak of God in this way,' they protest. 'He must remain absolutely transcendent; he must remain pure majesty. Majesty full of mercy, certainly, but not to the point of paying for the faults of his own creatures, for their sins'" (*Crossing the Threshold of Hope,* p. 41).

God reveals his name, his being, to Moses on Mount Horeb as an act of love for his people. God wants not so much to be known as to set his people free from slavery. At the very core of God's being is a powerful, powerful love. "In the course of its history, Israel was able to discover that God had only one reason to reveal himself to them, a single motive for choosing them from among all peoples as his special possession: his sheer gratuitous love" (*Catechism*, no. 218).

Our Lives Transformed

Read: *Catechism of the Catholic Church*, nos. 222-231

"Christian faith . . . is not simply a set of propositions to be accepted with intellectual assent. Rather, faith is lived knowledge of Christ, a living remembrance of his commandments, and a truth to be lived out."
– Pope John Paul, *The Splendor of Truth*, 88

"Believing in God, the only One, and loving him with all our being has enormous consequences for our whole life."
– *Catechism of the Catholic Church*, 222

When we begin to understand, really understand, who God is we are moved to live our lives in a new way.

Our God, the Yahweh God, is the source of everything that exists. God is I AM, the God who gives being. Without God, nothing would be. But God has chosen to create everything that is and to hold everything in being.

God is far, far beyond us and our understanding. Yet, God is very close to us. Meditating on our utter dependence on God can move one away from acting as though the world centred on me.

It can move a person to gratitude for God choosing to give me the gift of life and for giving the gifts of family and friends, of the natural world, of an ordered universe. As I sit in awe at these great gifts, I can see that the only proper response is to give everything back to God. But even if I give God everything, it pales next to what he has already given.

G. K. Chesterton writes, "It is the highest and holiest of paradoxes that the man who really knows he cannot pay his debt will be for ever paying it. . . . He will always be throwing things away into a bottomless pit of unfathomable thanks" (*St. Francis of Assisi*, p. 80).

In my gratitude, I can seek to make the best use of what God has provided. Instead of treating material objects as disposable, I experience them as God's gift. I seek not to dominate the natural world, but to treat material objects with utmost respect.

But, at the same time, I have an attitude of detachment to those objects. I do not gain my identity from my possessions for, if I do, those possessions have now possessed me. I gain my identity from God and I am merely the caretaker of objects.

Through my meditation on the Yahweh God, I come to know God's greatness and majesty. I gain a glimpse of the power of the God who created the roaring oceans, the vast expanse of the prairie, and the towering mountains. I am awed by the God whose mind can fathom every grain of sand on the sea shore. And I am overcome with emotion at the notion of a God who could manufacture the loving heart of a human person.

Indeed, we have God's promise that the human person is made in God's image and likeness. What great dignity has a person if he or she is like God! Such dignity must not be trampled on. It must be respected and nurtured so that it can become even more like God. Oh, how calloused we are in how we sometimes treat each other! We abuse the dignity of others in our idolatrous belief that we have some right to control others for our own good or pleasure. And yet there is also love.

In that love, we see but a shadow of the love of the God who made us and all that is. In such a loving God, we must trust. Even when times are tough, we trust. We know God made us out of love, not, as a sort of bad joke, for a life of futility. We can depend on God.

Trust and patience. These are not mere human virtues. They are attitudes to be expected in the person who knows God.

The life of a person who has come to understand the dependence of everything on God has a different quality than that of one who takes no note of God. It is awe-filled, grateful, respectful of other people and created things, and always trusts God.

This is not a moral superiority, but a different way of being.

Yet we don't always live up to this way of being. Too often, we are cynical, critical, indifferent, disrespectful. And when non-believers see that side of us, they are right to accuse us of hypocrisy.

For if we believe in this Yahweh God, our lives should be transformed. We will not merely think different thoughts, we will act different actions. We will live in a way so that Christ can be seen through us. Our lives will be transparent and the God who is the life of the world will shine through.

13

The Trinity:
A Community of Love

Read: *Catechism of the Catholic Church*, nos. 232-267

One of the remarkable things about the Catholic Church is that it is able to produce a 581-page compendium of doctrine when Jesus didn't teach much in the way of doctrine. He lived a life and, through his words and actions, gave us glimpses into the nature of God. But he didn't give us a structure of doctrine or of morality.

But does that mean that the *Catechism* is a human fabrication, mere opinions loosely related to the life and teachings of Christ? The Catholic answer to that is a definite "no." We maintain that the doctrines we propound today are the result of 2,000 years of collective reflection and judgment on what is contained in Scriptures. And we have the guarantee of Scripture itself that the church is "the pillar and bulwark of the truth" (1 Timothy 3:15).

When, for example, someone stated an opinion about the nature of God which seemed to be a new insight, the church reflected on that opinion in the light of Scripture to determine its truth. Sometimes, an erroneous opinion helped the church clarify its own point of view. The result was a new doctrine.

Perhaps this is most evident with the doctrine of the Trinity.

There are few direct references in Scripture to God as Father, Son and Holy Spirit and there is no reference to God as three persons sharing one divine nature. This understanding was developed in response to a fourth-century preacher named Arius.

Arius taught that Jesus was not God, but was created by God. Jesus did not exist from eternity, but although he was perfect, was created at a certain point in time. Arius' followers also maintained that the Holy Spirit was of lesser importance than either the Father or the Son, that he was God's servant.

This outlook was influential enough that the church called the Council of Nicea to deal with it. The final result was the Nicene Creed, an elaboration on the earlier Apostles' Creed, which was intended to dispel the Arian heresy.

Jesus, the church noted, had proclaimed his identity with God in statements such as "The Father and I are One" (John 10:30). Indeed, it was precisely these sorts of statements — blasphemy to the Jews — that spurred the Jewish leaders' determination to kill Jesus. Jesus' claim to be one with the Father was not a peripheral part of his ministry; it was the very core of his identity. Ultimately, one cannot say that Jesus was a good moral teacher, but not divine. Either admit that Jesus is one with the Father or denounce him as a mad fool.

As for the Holy Spirit, many New Testament passages testify to the Spirit's equality with the Father and the Son. Jesus' last words to his disciples, for example, were to "make disciples of all nations, baptizing them in the name of the Father and of the Son and of the Holy Spirit" (Matthew 28:19).

The church also rejected another heresy. Sabellius made the opposite mistake of Arius. Instead of downgrading Jesus, Sabellius denied that any distinction exists between the Father and the Son. The church again turned to Scripture and found Jesus saying, "I testify on my own behalf and the Father who sent me testifies on my behalf" (John 8:18).

Out of this process of reflection, the church came to speak of a God who is One, but composed of three distinct persons. It came to understand God not as a solitary God who has no experience of intimacy, but as a community of persons for whom love is the prime reality. This love is so boundless that it overflows into creation.

The church maintains that it is impossible to believe in the mystery of Christ — the Word made Flesh — without also believing the doctrine of the Trinity. And other doctrines, particularly those of grace and eternal life as our sharing in the life of God, are also incomprehensible unless we believe in God as Trinity.

Moreover, the doctrine of the Trinity has much to offer our war-like and wounded society. We suffer from a precarious quality to even the most intimate interpersonal relations, a dog-eat-dog ethic in economic life and a determination not to submit to any being greater than oneself. The harmony and love within the Trinity make it the perfect model for any human community, but especially for one rooted in rugged individualism. In particular, we have the example of Christ who "emptied himself, . . . humbled himself and became obedient" (Philippians 2:6-8).

But our efforts to imitate the Trinity in our families and other human communities are — as important as those efforts are — but a shadow of the more brilliant reality to which we are called. For we are made not just to be like God, but to share in his life. Through grace and in eternal life, we become God's adopted children, sharers in the very life of the Trinity. What precisely this means we now have but the faintest glimpses. But we do have Jesus' promise: "Those who love me will keep my word and my Father will love them, and we will come to them and make our home with them" (John 14:23).

14

The Father Almighty

Read: *Catechism of the Catholic Church*, nos. 268-278

Several years ago in Winnipeg, I picked up a young man who was hitchhiking a short distance. He saw the crucifix on the dashboard of my car and commented, "I don't believe in God anymore. I can't. I've seen too much suffering."

Sometimes, it's too much for the human mind to comprehend that a loving God would allow anyone to suffer, let alone experience the appalling atrocities we have seen in this century. How could an all-powerful, loving God allow the innocent to suffer?

The *Catechism of the Catholic Church* frankly admits, "Faith in God the Father Almighty can be put to the test by the experience of evil and suffering. God can sometimes seem to be absent and incapable of stopping evil. But in the most mysterious way God the Father has revealed his almighty power in the voluntary humiliation and resurrection of his Son, by which he conquered evil. . . .

"Only faith can embrace the mysterious ways of God's almighty power. This faith glories in its weaknesses in order to draw to itself God's power" (nos. 272-273).

We need, first of all, to view suffering in the context of human sin. Not, however, in the narrow, mechanistic way which says, "God will get you for that." Rather we must see suffering and evil as consequences of sin which has broken the unity between God and humanity and shattered the wholeness of creation.

Someone once told me how she asked a cab driver in a foreign country she was visiting why there was so much poverty there. His response was that the poor must have sinned and are now being punished for it.

This is a horrible image of a vengeful God. It is directly opposed to our Scriptures which describe how God holds a special place for the poor, even holds them next to his breast (Luke 16:23), and will leave the 99 saved ones behind in order to bring the lost sheep home. This is a God of unfathomable mercy, not of jealousy and vengefulness.

But neither must suffering be totally disconnected from sin and punishment. In a 1984 apostolic letter, Pope John Paul wrote that "Even if we must use great caution in judging human suffering as a consequence of concrete sins (this is shown precisely by the example of the just man Job), nevertheless suffering cannot be divorced from the sin of the beginnings, from what St. John calls 'the sin of the world.' . . . At the basis of human suffering there is a complex involvement with sin" (*On the Christian Meaning of Human Suffering,* 15).

Even earthquakes and tornadoes — random "acts of God" — are a consequence of sin. Because humanity is not at peace with God, the earth itself rebels.

But our exploration of suffering must go deeper still if we are to fathom this mystery.

We cannot make peace with the mystery of suffering by remaining outside faith, by suspending judgment about the existence of a loving God in order to reach a reasoned judgment about the "facts." The only way to begin to understand this mystery is to first accept that God is real and loving.

With an acceptance of the amazing truth that not only does God refuse to abolish suffering, but that he became human in order to share in our suffering as the most totally innocent victim, we can begin to enter into the meaning of suffering.

Our suffering can only be understood in the light of Christ's suffering. Jesus Christ has saved the world through his suffering. We can share in that act of salvation through a free acceptance of our own suffering. In his apostolic letter, the pope described suffering as "something good, before which the church bows down in reverence with all the depth of her faith in the redemption" (no. 24).

This is a shocking statement. Suffering good? Isn't suffering evil, something which should be avoided at all costs? When I first experienced the power of the Holy Spirit, I thought God was going to heal me and make me happier. I thought God was going to take away all suffering, "wipe every tear from their eyes" (Revelation 21:4).

We should try to end suffering, especially suffering inflicted on others. But suffering need not be useless. In the cosmic battle of good against evil, the pope wrote, "human sufferings, united to the redemptive suffering of Christ, constitute a special support for the powers of good, and open the way to the victory of these salvific powers" (no. 27).

One of the paradoxes of Christian living is that it is through our acceptance of suffering that human suffering can finally be brought to an end.

If I was confronted by that young hitchhiker again today, I would tell him to look at that crucifix on the dashboard. I would tell him that

that is God hanging there on the cross, the almighty God who he wants to end all suffering. I would tell him that if God will freely suffer for us then we should be willing to suffer for God and for others. Moreover, our sufferings can have merit. We should ask God to use our sufferings for the final defeat of evil.

The Creator of the Universe

Read: *Catechism of the Catholic Church*, nos. 279-354

The origin of the created world is one of the great universal puzzles or mysteries. Every society or religion has tried to penetrate the mystery of where everything came from.

So-called primitive peoples told stories to explain the mystery. One such myth — attributed to West Coast aboriginal people — tells of how the first woman created the first boy out of her own mucous. Scientists, meanwhile, develop theories which attempt to explain the empirical data about the earth's beginnings. Today we talk of the Big Bang and biological evolution.

Neither myth nor science, however, answers the more fundamental question: Why is there something rather than nothing? Moreover, the world has an apparent moral dimension which raises another question: Why does this world in which we live contain both good and evil?

One of the more enduring attempts to answer these questions was that of the third-century Persian philosopher, Mani. For Mani and his followers, the Manicheans, there is a principle of goodness and light, and a principle of evil and darkness. These two forces are autonomous of each other and are continually at war.

For Mani, our world, especially the human person, contains a mixture of good and evil. But matter itself and human desires are essentially evil. The role of the Manichean is to separate the light from the darkness by living an ascetic life, especially by avoiding procreation.

Some of this sounds vaguely Christian. Perhaps that's due to our exposure to too many bad movies which picture Catholicism as a world-hating religion interested almost exclusively in driving the devil out of lustful young hearts. Moreover, Manicheanism has been a tendency within the church itself which ebbs and flows, but never totally disappears. The real question is the extent to which the identification of the flesh with evil represents the church's teaching.

In fact, every time a world-hating sect like Manicheanism, Albigensianism or Jansenism has arisen, the church has fought it tooth and nail.

For there are few things more at odds with Christian revelation than the view that the material world is evil.

The first two chapters of Genesis say over and over that God created everything in the universe and that it is all good. At the end of his creating, "God saw everything that he had made, and indeed, it was very good" (Genesis 1:31).

The church's great hymn Te Deum — part of the daily Liturgy of the Hours — proclaims, "You are the eternal Father: all creation worships you." How could an evil creation worship a good God?

The Manicheans despised marriage and procreation. The church calls marriage a sacrament and rejoices in the beginning of another human life.

At the very heart of Christian revelation is the Word-made-Flesh. God did not simply send messengers to humanity, he became human. Nothing could be a stronger affirmation of the sacredness of the material world. The Catholic faith is not a soul-destroying faith, but rather one which praises life and calls on us to live life to the fullest.

It is here that we find the rub. For living life to the fullest does not mean indulging all our appetites indiscriminately. For if that were the case then addictions would be the highest form of praising God, not simply a tawdry type of idolatry.

And so, in one form or another, we ought to deny ourselves as a way of adoring God. We fast in order to discipline our appetites. We also fast so as to share in the sufferings of Jesus Christ. Such asceticism is a reminder of our own utter poverty — that we depend on God for everything. If we find salvation it is not through our own efforts, but as a free gift of God.

Unlike the fasting of the Manicheans, Christian self-denial is not about destroying what God has created. It is not self-sterilization, but part of the growth towards fruitfulness. It is a way of allowing the life of the vine to flow into us, its branches.

Because everything in creation is God's choice, not the happenstance result of a furious Star Wars-type battle, God cares for everything in the world. God does not despise what he has made. We too should love creation and should use it to give glory to God.

However, the world, as we well know, is not perfect. Our machines break down, our plans are interrupted by a family crisis, and we get sick, suffer and die. The world is, as the *Catechism* states, "'in a state of journeying' towards an ultimate perfection yet to be attained, to which God has destined it" (no. 302).

This "state of journeying" can be a source of frustration and grief. But knowing that we are on a journey is quite different from believing that our lives are being cast about on an ocean of turmoil caused by an unpredictable battle between the forces of good and evil. The Christian view allows us to live in trust and in hope and calls us to respect the dignity of each person.

For built into our outlook is a confidence in ultimate victory over the forces of evil who, while always banging at the door, are no match for the power of God.

16

The Human Person: Made in God's Image

Read: *Catechism of the Catholic Church*, nos. 355-384

In some circles, the story is often told of a village of people who lived on a river. One day, their peaceful existence was interrupted by the body of a dying woman floating in the river.

The people of the village took her ashore and cared for her until her death. As time passed, more and more bodies floated down the river. Finally, one soul decided to go upstream to find and deal with the cause of this tragedy.

The point of the story is that it is far better to eradicate the root causes of suffering than to bandage up the victims of injustice. As far as it goes, this is an important point. There is much structural injustice in the world and part of loving one's neighbour is to change those structures.

But the story can also leave us looking down our noses at some of the great saints of our time. Why is Mother Teresa praised for tending to the dying beggars of Calcutta without questioning the structures which leave so many impoverished? Why did Cardinal Paul-Émile Léger abandon a position of power and influence to live with lepers in Cameroon? Why do we laud Jean Vanier for living with mentally handicapped people when, with his brains and contacts, he could have fought successfully for lasting improvements in living conditions for these people?

Why, indeed, did Jesus choose to heal some, but only some, of the blind, the lame and the sick in first-century Palestine?

Were these people too naive to challenge the structures of injustice? Or were they, while seeing the injustice, perhaps trying to do something even more important?

By holding one person close, one of the least among us, these saints affirm the dignity of all. The worth of a person is not determined by how much he or she can contribute to or draw from the gross national product. Human dignity is totally unearned, it is the result of being a child of God. It is a gift.

It is a gift given to us because we are more than flesh and blood. A person, states the *Catechism*, is "not just something, but someone" (no. 357). Humanity "alone is called to share, by knowledge and love, in God's own life" (no. 356).

A person is not just a body. Nor is a person a soul hitched to a body, a body which prevents one from realizing his or her dignity. Rather, the unity of body and soul is "profound" — "it is because of its spiritual soul that the body made of matter becomes a living, human body" (no. 365).

So the work of Mother Teresa is not so much that of patching up nameless bodies hauled in off the street. It is true that these are beggars who are not likely to rebound from their condition to write great musical scores, discover the cure for cancer or invent new home appliances.

But despite that, their human dignity is every bit as great as those who will do those things. Their dignity comes not from their usefulness, but because they are created in the image of the Triune God.

In fact, it is in our weaknesses that our dignity is most evident. This is the opposite of what we often think. When our pride and usefulness is stripped away, we stand naked before God in all our poverty and foolishness, but also in our glory as children of God.

Mother Teresa is not an advocate for social justice. She is something more basic than that — she is a witness to irreducible dignity of each human person, a dignity which itself is a testimony of the greatness of God.

But neither does the love of a Mother Teresa undermine the quest for justice. In fact, it makes justice a possibility.

The secular quest for social justice has too often mirrored that which it fights against — it has too often treated people as means to an end. The result has been new forms of violence and oppression. But justice rooted in love of each person and respect for each person's dignity will never resort to oppression.

In Edmonton, one of our great advocates for social justice, Mary Burlie, died in the summer of 1996. At her funeral, numerous people came forward to speak of how Mary had touched their lives, indeed, had altered their lives for the better. Mary believed in people whom everyone else had cast aside. She had loved them and hung in with them when times were tough.

It was clear that Mary's outspoken advocacy for social justice grew out of her love for real people, hundreds of them. She went upstream. But her advocacy was the fruit of love, not ideology. By opening her heart to the oppressed, Mary's life became a powerful testimony to the love of God and the dignity of the human person.

17

Sin: Original Harmony Shattered

Read: *Catechism of the Catholic Church*, nos. 385-421

As a teenager, I came to believe that the rules and discipline imposed on children and youth by adults were the greatest impediment to the free flowering of the human person.

Freed from the tyranny of having to conform to the conventions of straight society, children would naturally be not only uninhibited, but also more loving and caring than anyone today could imagine. The best form of political organization was anarchy and the highest human virtue was spontaneity.

I read a lot of respected political and psychological thinkers who, in one way or another, shared my point of view and who thus encouraged me on my merry way.

Every once in a while, I would trip over an author like Plato or St. Augustine who had a decidedly different understanding of the human person. Both of them saw the human person as having a somewhat devilish nature which needed to be reined in. But I brushed them aside as fascists who were driven by guilt and suspicion.

I'm not sure what changed my mind on this — even 10 years ago I was reading Matthew Fox's theory of "original blessing" somewhat uncritically. Perhaps I just began to realize how badly children are cheated when their parents leave them to their own devices and how an uncritical worship of spontaneity has undermined the child-rearing process in Western society.

I haven't done a total turn-around on this issue. But now with two young children of my own, I think one of the greatest gifts I can give them is the respectful imposition of limits. Limits on their behaviour and limits on the number of their possessions. They will chafe at the bit and they may never be grateful for having those limits imposed on them, but they will, nevertheless, be better people for being reined in.

Some wag once described a neoconservative as a radical with a teenage daughter. There's more than a little truth here. Even if your are blasé about your own safety and moral character, you're bound to be concerned about the proper nurturing of your children.

The *Catechism* talks about the "harmony of original justice" (no. 379) in God's creation. We are created good, not evil. But evil sneaks into the picture as humanity refuses to accept the few limits God has placed on it. This failure to trust in God is breached by one human action. The action shatters the original harmony and the world is "inundated by sin" (no. 401).

The *Catechism* says the story of Adam and Eve is a figurative one, told to explicate the mystery of lawlessness among God's people. But while the story is not literally true, what is essential is that there was "a primeval event," an actual historical deed through which humanity turned its back on God (no. 390).

The prospects for humanity would be bleak if Jesus had not come on the scene. There would be no way out of the maze of sin without Christ's act of redemption. Our own actions will never lift us out of dust; we can only be saved by the power of God. But even though Christ offers us the possibility of salvation, human nature remains "weak and inclined to evil" (no. 405).

Sin is real. Evil is not simply the result of poor social conditioning or a bad upbringing. Each person carries the tendency not just to goof up, but to consciously and deliberately turn away from God.

We need good social programs and improved parenting. But these will not usher in a new heaven and a new earth. Sin and evil will persist until the final trumpet blows.

In his encyclical *Centesimus Annus,* Pope John Paul drew the notion of original sin into the discussion of social and political issues. "The human person tends towards good, but is also capable of evil," he said.

"When people think they possess the secret of a perfect social organization which makes evil impossible, they also think they can use any means, including violence and deceit, in order to bring that organization into being. . . . No political society . . . can ever be confused with the kingdom of God" (no. 25).

Christians are not engaged in building Utopia, but in an ongoing spiritual battle against the powers of darkness and temptation. Our hope comes through Christ as the source of grace. Trust in God and reliance on that grace are our main weapons in the spiritual battle. They were the virtues missing in the act of original sin and they are what will help restore the harmony that was shattered.

18

Jesus Christ:
The Centre of History

Read: *Catechism of the Catholic Church*, nos. 422-429

Viewed from the outside, there is a certain arrogance to the Christian position. This apparent arrogance lies in the assertion that in the great ocean of people, time and events, there is one person and one event which is the hinge on which everything else turns.

Isn't the life, death and resurrection of Jesus Christ just a faded memory, a relic from long ago which has little meaning for us today? Or, aren't the life and teachings of Moses, Mohammed, Buddha or Confucius of equal importance to that of the carpenter who was executed 2,000 years ago on a garbage dump? Isn't it presumptuous to say Jesus is the centre of all history?

We have spoken of God the Father from whom all life, all creation comes. If God is the Father then why is there a need for the Son? And if there is God the Son, why does he become flesh at one, limited point in history? Indeed, this is what we believe — that the God who has created and sustained all history has also become one of the billions of people who participate in that history.

In this life, we will never be able to fully plumb the mystery of the Trinity, to fully know the why of the three persons. But we do know that the heart of God is love, a love that is lived out within the communion of three persons. And, through the revelation given to us by Jesus Christ, we know that we are made to share in that communion.

God is not a solitary God, but the Trinity. And this tells something of utmost importance about our own salvation. For if there were no distinction of persons in the Godhead then salvation could only consist of our being totally absorbed into God, thus losing our individuality. But salvation through Christ consists of entering into communion with God, becoming one with God while retaining our own personhood.

Jesus is crucial to salvation. During the Preparation of the Gifts at Mass, the priest says, "By the mystery of this water and wine may we come to share in the divinity of Christ, who humbled himself to share in our humanity."

Jesus is the one mediator between God and humanity who, by becoming human, paved the way for us to share in divine life. Jesus told the apostle Thomas, "No one comes to the Father except through me" (John 14:6).

Before Jesus' death and resurrection, this was not possible. One could live a good life and follow God's laws. Maybe after such a life, one could go to a happy hunting ground. But no one, without Jesus, could share in divine life.

St. Paul writes that "whenever Moses is read, a veil lies over their minds; but when one turns to the Lord, the veil is removed" (2 Corinthians 3:15-16). God shines "in our hearts to give the light of the knowledge of the glory of God in the face of Jesus Christ" (2 Corinthians 4:6).

Christians should never attempt to impose faith on others. But we have an obligation to make others aware of the new life that can be gained through Christ. The *Catechism* says, "The transmission of the Christian faith consists primarily in proclaiming Jesus Christ in order to lead others to faith in him. From the beginning, the first disciples burned with the desire to proclaim Christ" (no. 425).

So must we. We must come to know this person who is the centre of human history. Jesus Christ is not a dusty memory, but a living reality. We must hear his story, make it our own and share it with others. This is the only real hope for ourselves and our only real hope for the world.

19

The Holy Names of Jesus Christ

Read: *Catechism of the Catholic Church*, nos. 430-455

At first glance, it may seem odd that while Jesus sometimes calls himself the Son of Man, he never referred to himself as the Christ, the Messiah. And when Peter recognized Jesus as the Christ, the Son of the living God, Jesus ordered the disciples not to tell anyone.

Jesus' hesitation to be known as the Messiah stems from the Jewish belief that the Messiah would be a great worldly ruler, a glorious king. The title Son of Man, however, has Scriptural links with the Suffering Servant described by the prophet Isaiah. Jesus' mission was to suffer, not to run the government.

In this light, it makes sense that Jesus would tell the disciples not to spread the word that he is the Messiah. It would create false expectations. Indeed, Peter himself had such expectations. Suffering and death "must never happen to you," he told the Lord (Matthew 16:22).

Perhaps it seems unusual that the writers of the *Catechism* would devote a section to the names and titles by which Jesus was known in Scripture — Jesus, Christ, the only Son of God, the Lord. But each of those names helps us to understand the divine nature of Jesus Christ. The first act of a Christian is to know and love Jesus. So, by coming to a greater awareness of the names by which he was known, we can draw closer to him.

The name Jesus means "God saves." Even in his given name, there is a sign of Jesus' mission. Just as God led his people out of Egypt, so Jesus will save us from sin.

The word "Christ" (Messiah) means the anointed one. Although Jesus was reluctant to be known publicly as the Christ, he was aware of his identity as Messiah. His role as the Christ is to establish God's kingdom on earth. But this is a different sort of kingdom. "The true meaning of his kingship is revealed only when he is raised high on the cross" (*Catechism*, no. 440).

At both Jesus' baptism and his transfiguration, the voice of the Father designates Jesus as his "beloved Son." All of us are called to live

as adopted children of God. But Jesus' sonship is even more intimate —
he is the only begotten Son of the Father.

Jesus is also known as the Lord, the same name which the Hebrews
used to refer to Yahweh. The term "'Lord' expresses the recognition of
the divine mystery of Jesus" (no. 448). It also implies that we should not
submit our personal freedom to anyone or anything but Jesus.

By reflecting on these different names or titles given to Jesus we
can understand better who he is. Jesus is given other titles in the New
Testament which are not dealt with so thoroughly by the *Catechism* —
titles such as the Good Shepherd, the new Adam and the Bread of Life.
These can also help us understand Jesus.

But the church has traditionally seen the name of Jesus as imparting
more than understanding. It sees power in the name itself.

After Pentecost, Peter healed a crippled man when he said, "In the
name of Jesus Christ of Nazareth, stand up and walk" (Acts 3:6).

In later centuries, beginning with the early church fathers, devotion
to the holy name developed and miracles were attributed to the
prayerful invocation of Jesus' name.

This devotion reached a peak with St. Bernadine of Siena in the fif-
teenth century. Bernadine gave sermons aiming to spur a strong love for
and devotion to the name of Jesus. At the end of his sermons, the saint
held high a tablet bearing the Lord's name in letters of gold. Some saw
this practice as idolatrous, but it eventually received wholehearted
approval from the pope of the day.

In our day, such practices and devotions might seem hokey. However, they should challenge us to examine the ways in which speech and
images are used in our culture. All too often, we see the spoken word as
something ephemeral, as lacking in staying power. We fail to see how
one's style of speech reflects what is in the person's heart and how
words can alter and define the character of those who use them and
those who receive them. Words should not be used carelessly.

Our speech, our reading and writing, and the TV programs and
movies we choose to watch can be a way to raise up or lower our own
dignity. Understood in that light, the reverent use of the holy name of
Jesus can be an important way for us to participate in building up God's
kingdom.

20

Truly God, Truly Human

Read: *Catechism of the Catholic Church*, nos. 456-483

"He's a man, he's just a man."
– Jesus Christ Superstar

The earliest heresies in the Christian Church came from those who couldn't believe that God actually became human. They believed that, in some sort of divine trick, Jesus only appeared to be human.

Part of the basis for this belief was the corruptibility, indeed the profanity, of all that is physical. God, in the view of these people (known as Docetists), could never be lowered into the physical realm. God would defy, and defile, his own nature to become human like us.

This heresy was formally condemned by the Council of Chalcedon in the year 451. But it has lived on over the ages, not so much in its purest form as in other forms of hatred of the flesh.

Jansenism, for example, didn't teach that Jesus was a spirit who only appeared to be a body. But it denied the existence of a human ability to cooperate with God's grace to achieve salvation. For the Jansenists, one's eternal fate is predestined because human flesh does not have the capacity for acts of will which can make a difference. Nevertheless, people of this conviction made enormous efforts to crucify their own flesh to give a sign that they had been saved.

The second round of heresies came from those who contended that while Jesus was surely human, he wasn't quite God. These heresies took form in various movements — such as the Arians and Nestorians — which were also formally condemned by a string of church councils in the fourth through the sixth centuries.

The problem here wasn't hatred of the flesh and the world. In fact, it may have been an overly trusting attitude towards the human will. Jesus, after all, was seen as deeply linked to God, even if he was essentially human. For the Arians, we could achieve salvation through our own actions, almost apart from anything God did.

Again, we see a tendency which continues to this day. Although few practising Catholics would assert that Jesus is a man but not God, popular portrayals such as *Jesus Christ Superstar* and *Godspell* do cast him in such a way.

What has been refreshing in the post-Vatican II church is that many Catholics — primarily by paying greater attention to the Gospels — have recovered a sense of the humanity of Jesus. Jesus has become more real, more personal, someone with whom one can have a relationship.

But there is a danger in being so focused on Jesus our brother that we lose sight that Jesus is Lord. It must be noted that Jansenism began as a reforming movement within a church that had grown spiritually lax. Its desire to restore a strong sense of the otherness of the divine and the fallenness of humanity is a legitimate one, one which unfortunately was carried to extremes.

From the above description, it should be clear that our attitudes towards Jesus' divinity and his humanity are related to how we view the human person and to how we act. If one sees the human body as an unholy cesspool of desires, it may mean one has grasped the transcendence of Jesus, but is out of touch with his humanity.

If one sees the human person as intrinsically good to the point where sin is almost out of the picture, then one likely sees Jesus, if one sees him at all, as our brother, but has little grasp of him as our saviour and redeemer.

Pope John Paul deals with this issue in his 1991 encyclical *Mission of the Redeemer*. The pope worries about the current tendency towards "the gradual secularization of salvation" (no. 11). In his view, we today are threatened more by the tendency to view the person purely in "horizontal" terms than by an overemphasis on the "vertical" relationship with the transcendent God.

If the pope is right, we can expect a Jansenist-type reaction to follow. An over-emphasis in one direction is surely followed by an over-emphasis in the other.

But the pope says we ought to focus on "integral salvation" — roughly defined as saving both the body and the soul. This full salvation offers us the possibility of becoming God's adopted children.

We ought to strive for a balance in our understanding of who Jesus is. The *Catechism of the Catholic Church* gives us a simple, but rich, formula for keeping that balance: "He became truly man while remaining truly God. Jesus Christ is true God and true man" (no. 464).

21

Made Incarnate of the Virgin Mary

Read: *Catechism of the Catholic Church*, nos. 484-495

The royal doors in the icon screen in Byzantine churches tradition-ally include an icon of the Annunciation — that moment when Mary accepted the angel's request for her to become the Mother of God.

This well-considered placement of the icon of the Annunciation shows that moment in history when humanity's options were forever transformed. The incarnation made it possible for the people who walked in darkness to enter through those royal doors into God's kingdom of unsurpassed light.

The church's teaching about Mary the Mother of God has been much misunderstood. It has been maintained that the church has deified Mary, turned her into an idol crowding the Son of God from his throne. Some see the church as having taken the so-called feminine qualities of God and projected them onto Mary. As such, the church treats her as a goddess, an earth mother, a holdover from pagan fertility cults.

Perhaps Catholic piety has occasionally provided some basis for those assertions. But the church's teaching has sought not to glorify Mary, but to help us understand her role in the process of a salvation which comes through Jesus Christ alone. As the *Catechism of the Catholic Church* states, "What the Catholic Church believes about Mary is based on what it believes about Christ, and what it teaches about Mary illumines in turn its faith in Christ" (no. 487).

Indeed, efforts through history to downplay Mary's role in salva-tion were often linked to a lack of faith in Jesus. For example, the fifth-century heretic Nestorius insisted on addressing Mary as the mother of Christ, not the Mother of God *(Theotokos)*. That insistence was linked to the Arians' denial of Christ's divinity.

Nor was Mary's acceptance of God's will akin to her saying, "OK! I'll let you use my body for nine months and yes, I will raise the child." It was something far deeper than that. There was no separation of body from spirit in Mary.

Indeed, it has been rightly said that she conceived Jesus in her soul before she received him into her womb. Her declaration to Elizabeth that "My soul magnifies the Lord and my spirit rejoices in God my Saviour" (Luke 1:47) testifies to her total turning over of herself to the will of God. The Mother of God heard and kept God's word in every aspect of her being.

If Mary was not a surrogate mother for Jesus, that also tells us something about Jesus. Mary was not just the mother of Jesus' body, but of his whole person. He took human flesh from her and his divine nature from the Holy Spirit. But he was not half-God and half-human. Nor was he born as a human who later became divine. Jesus was always full human and fully divine, united in one person.

When the Council of Ephesus (431) took on Nestorius and declared Mary to be the Mother of God, that was the truth it wished to defend — that Jesus is truly God and truly human.

Moreover, the church is also telling us that the second person is not just the Logos of the philosophers, but also Jesus who walked among us and was warmed by a mother's love. God is very close to us, closer than we might dare to imagine.

In terms of our salvation, Mary's motherhood enabled God's Son to become one of us so that we could be God's adopted children. "And because you are children, God has sent the Spirit of his Son into our hearts" (Galatians 4:6). We thus owe an immense debt of gratitude to Mary because of what her faith has meant for us. Later, the *Catechism* will examine this notion of Mary as the spiritual mother of the church (no. 964-975).

Ultimately, the significance of Mary as the Mother of God is that, like her, humanity is called to collaborate with God. God did not impose himself upon her; she freely chose to allow her life to be used for God's purposes.

Because Mary was free of the inclination to selfishness wrought by original sin (her immaculate conception), she was better able to let God's light be seen than are we. But we too are called to be handmaids of the Lord, to be nothing so that Christ can be everything. And to the extent that we succeed, we too deserve a place on the royal doors through which others can enter into God's marvellous light.

22

The "Obsession" with Mary's Virginity

Read: *Catechism of the Catholic Church*, nos. 496-511

The church has received considerable ridicule over the centuries for proclaiming the perpetual virginity of Mary. This is a doctrine which has been seen as promoting sexual repression and as having forced women to strive after the impossible goal of being both virgins and mothers.

Yet, despite all the scorn the church has received for this doctrine, it continues to insist on both its truth and its importance for our lives. Why are we so hung up on Mary's virginity?

In fact, Mary's virginity is not about sexual morality, but about grace, about how God comes to us in our lowliness.

Mary's virginal conception needs to be seen in the context of other miraculous births in Jewish history. It must be seen in the tradition of the birth of Isaac to Sarah (Genesis 12), the birth of Samuel to Hannah (1 Samuel 1-3), the birth of Samson (Judges 13) and the birth of John to Elizabeth (Luke 1).

In each of these cases, God does the impossible thing — he blesses an elderly, barren woman with a child who will do great things among God's people. Each of these women was a woman of great faith, faith which persisted in spite of the lack of a sign from God. But because of both their faith and the gratuitous action of God, their barrenness became an abundant source of life.

These biblical stories were literally true. But their greatest significance is as signs of how God's grace can transform times of humiliation into occasions for rejoicing. We must look deeper than the physical facts to find the symbolic truth.

The doctrine of the virginal conception was never questioned in the early church. The doctrine was seen as a sign of Jesus' divine origin, a sign that the initiative in Jesus' conception lay totally with God. God reaches out to a woman with an offer of the greatest gift possible — to bear the Son of God. This holy offer is given to Mary because it is she who has the deepest sense of unconditional receptivity, of humble acceptance of this offer.

Indeed, we need to be constantly reminded of this: we do not make our own salvation; we receive it as a gift from God. Grace always enters humanity this way, as totally unearned. We need a listening heart to receive it. Such a listening heart requires an acceptance of our lowliness, a renunciation of the human will to power.

But the church also asserts that Jesus was born virginally. In a way we don't understand, Mary's virginity remained intact through the birth of Jesus. Some see this doctrine as evidence of a male-dominated church's obsession with female virginity. Viewed from a purely secular outlook, that objection is understandable.

The Eastern churches, however, especially emphasize the virgin birth as a sign of the new creation found in Jesus Christ. They draw our attention to the symbolism of Mary as the new Eve whose obedience overcame the punishments wrought by Eve's disobedience.

They point to Genesis 3:16 — "To the woman, the Lord God said, 'I will greatly increase your pangs in childbearing, in pain you shall bring forth children, yet your desire shall be for your husband, and he shall rule over you."

In that statement, they see the punishment God gave to women which is shattered at the Nativity. The birth of Jesus anticipates our redemption and, as such, Mary was freed from the pangs of birth *and* from patriarchy.

The early church also saw the virgin birth as a symbolic anticipation of the resurrection in another way. Christ's birth from the unbroken womb was symbolic of his emerging from the closed sepulchre. In the virgin birth, we thus see a sign of Christ's ultimate triumph over death.

Finally, the church holds that Mary remained a virgin forever. Certainly, it cannot be reasonably held that Mary could have given birth to the Son of God and have remained unchanged as a person. We believe that her commitment to God was always total. But with the Annunciation, she was transformed further — she became the spouse of the Holy Spirit. So we can understand Mary as freely choosing to remain a perpetual virgin out of love for God.

St. Augustine maintained that Mary had made such a choice even before the Annunciation. He pointed to her statement to the angel — "How can this be, since I am a virgin" (Luke 1:34) — as an indication that she had already committed herself to remain a perpetual virgin.

The church does hold Mary up as a model for women especially to imitate. On the feast of the Assumption in 1995, Pope John Paul said, "In Mary, virgin and mother, femininity finds its full expression, because in her the personal qualities that distinguish women from men were manifest in all their splendour.''

But the church does not expect the impossible — it does not condemn women for failing to be both virgins and mothers. Nor does it maintain that virginity is necessary to sanctity. Indeed, the church holds marriage and childbearing in high esteem.

Mary, moreover, is also the prime example for men. All Christians are called to act out of an awareness that we are the unworthy recipients of salvation, made possible by the death and resurrection of God's Only Son. Mary shows all of us the way to Jesus.

23

The Life of Christ

Read: *Catechism of the Catholic Church*, nos. 512-570

Catholics are frequently told that the paschal mystery of Christ's death and resurrection is the centre of our faith. Everything hangs on the truth and the power of that mystery.

If Christ did not rise from the dead, then our faith is in vain. The wages of sin is death and if Christ has not conquered death, he has not conquered sin. He has failed to redeem humanity.

All of this is true and of utmost importance but, I suspect, of little help to a person who is on the outside of the faith, daring to wonder whether to step in.

For what draws one to faith is the person of Jesus. Here is a man who, 2,000 years after he walked among us, continues to exert an almost magnetic attraction for those who read and grapple with the Gospels. In Jesus, we have not a philosopher, but a man of the purest simplicity and goodness.

No one who reads the Gospels can ignore the way Jesus reached out and performed remarkable acts of healing and kindness for those forgotten ones who came to him — beggars, prostitutes, lepers, sick and elderly women. In the ways they most needed help, Jesus helped them when they asked and sought no publicity for himself.

John and Denise Carmody write, "Much of the appeal of Jesus has lain in his ability to touch wounded hearts. People down on themselves, finding they were no good or had no future, could hear in his preaching a gentle counsel to never lose heart.

"Jesus did not tell them that they were not really so bad or that they haven't made themselves morally ugly. They wouldn't have believed that and Jesus didn't try to make them.

"His tack rather was to tell them that God did not much care about moral beauty or ugliness, that God's love was predicated on something far more intrinsic and profound. For Jesus, God loves each creature as only its parents love a child or its maker loves a product.

"God finally is moved to search people out and to heal people's wounds because that is God's own makeup: utter goodness, never-failing creativity and love" (*Jesus: An Introduction,* pp. 150-151).

We can't brush aside Jesus' public ministry as just a warm-up for the really good stuff. When, after the death of Judas and Christ's resurrection, the apostles sought a replacement for Judas among the 12, they were careful who they chose.

They would not settle for one who was a witness to the resurrection. They sought "one of the men who have accompanied us during all the time that the Lord Jesus went in and out among us, beginning from the baptism of John until the day when he was taken up from us" (Acts 1:21-22).

This new apostle had to have walked with Jesus throughout his public ministry. He had to have seen the miracles and heard the teaching.

No doubt one reason for this requirement was that it was important that the twelfth apostle have received the missionary training and teaching that Jesus provided to those closest to him. But, more importantly, the apostle would have had to know Jesus well as a person.

Indeed, this is where our faith is made or broken — on our response to the person of Jesus. Is Jesus someone we can follow from his baptism to Calvary? And, if we follow him, who do we say he is?

As they journeyed with Jesus the disciples had trouble deciding who he was. Many were impressed that Jesus was not a mere interpreter of God's word, but that he spoke as one with authority. But that awareness did not itself bring them to faith in Christ's divinity. Something more was needed.

It was Peter who made the first leap of Christian faith when he told Jesus: "You are the Messiah, the Son of the living God." This, before the crucifixion and before the resurrection. This, based on, but also more than, Peter's intimate knowledge of Jesus as a person. "Flesh and blood has not revealed this to you," Jesus responded to Peter, "but my Father in heaven" (Matthew 16:16-17).

With this proclamation of faith, everything changes. Now we head towards the cross and the resurrection. With a full knowledge of Jesus' identity, the final stages of the mystery of Jesus' redemption can take place. Now that we know God is fully our brother, we can receive the further revelation — that he will take our sins upon his shoulder and die for us. And by dying and rising, he will enable us to be one with him.

When we look back over Jesus' life through the prism of the resurrection, everything will look different, be shot through with fuller meaning than it had before we knew how Christ was to conquer death. The virgin birth, the wedding at Cana, the woman at the well — the meaning of these and other events will all be clearer and richer for us than before the resurrection. But to come to believe in the resurrection we will first need to come to know Jesus, the man from Galilee.

24

Jesus the Revolutionary

Read: *Catechism of the Catholic Church*, nos. 571-598

Occasionally in popular culture, one encounters portrayals of Jesus as a sort of first-century rebel insurrectionist. In this view, Jesus got in trouble with Jewish authorities for being an outside agitator who travelled around the country and worked people up for a revolution called the kingdom of God. He was a subversive and non-conformist who consorted with all varieties of sinners.

More than 25 years ago, I had a "wanted" poster for Jesus in my high school locker accusing him of being such an outlaw. It was a convenient way to glorify my own insubordination, a rather self-serving way of putting Jesus in a new light.

In fact, when popular culture bothers to pay attention to Jesus, this is often how it paints him. Such portrayals tend to be a way of justifying one's own abandonment of any standards of morality and behaviour. One can use Jesus as a supposed model of irreverence and individualism.

In this outlook, any defenders of tradition are, at least by implication, cast as grim forces of darkness who repress the spontaneous and non-conformist forces of light and gaiety. They're rigid, narrow and anti-creative. They will delay the inevitable arrival of the Age of Aquarius.

It needs to be said that, while this picture contains shards of truth, it presents basically a false Jesus. And it is important to say this now because Western society is falling into decay partly due to a widespread and growing individualism, an individualism which is determined to portray morality as repression.

Jesus was a strong individual — a man with a clear sense of his vocation and a determination to carry it out with integrity. But he was not an individualist. He came to do the Father's will, not his own. The carrying out of his mission was not a matter of self-aggrandizement, an excuse for abandoning moral standards.

The *Catechism of the Catholic Church* describes a Jesus who was far from being in direct opposition to the religious establishment of Israel. In fact, he endorsed many of its teachings. He insisted on keeping the Mosaic law down to "the least of these commandments" (Matthew 5:19) and "expressed the greatest respect for the Temple in Jerusalem" (*Catechism*, no. 583).

Jesus did, however, get under the skin of the leaders of a most diverse collection of Jewish movements by making the Sabbath prohibitions of the law secondary to the law of love, by teaching "as one who had authority" (Matthew 7:28), by identifying himself with the Temple and by announcing that the Temple would be destroyed. According to the *Catechism*, "Jesus gave scandal above all when he identified his merciful conduct toward sinners with God's own attitude toward them" (no. 589).

Jewish leaders wanted Jesus executed because he was a blasphemer (no. 591). His "blasphemy," however, was a simple, humble faithfulness to the mission his Father gave him. He knew such fidelity could only bring him suffering and eventually death.

For Jesus, the Jewish law was far from being a form of repression. It was something that he came to fulfil. The problem was human weakness — people are incapable of carrying out the details of the law on their own initiative, whether it be the Mosaic law or natural moral law. It is only by sharing in the divine life of God as his adopted children that we can fulfil the law. And it was Christ's cross and resurrection that made it possible for us to enter into that divine life.

The opposition between Jesus and the Jewish leaders is far from being as stark as it is sometimes portrayed. While the acts of some Jewish leaders which led to Jesus' death may have been seriously sinful, they cannot be cast as a monolithic force repressing the human spirit. Jesus himself was in agreement with much that they taught.

The lesson for our culture is that non-conformity, individualism and irreverence towards religious authority are steps in the wrong direction. They do not move us towards Jesus. What we ought to do is live as Jesus lived — with total integrity and in total obedience to the will of the Father.

25

Jesus Makes Good for Our Sins

Read: *Catechism of the Catholic Church*, nos. 599-623

Disgusted to read in the morning paper that the Oilers have traded his favorite hockey player to the Flames, George throws the piece of toast he is eating across the kitchen, catching his wife Margaret square in the forehead. He then storms off to work, muttering to himself.

Later, George is embarrassed by what he has done. So, he considers several possible courses of action to make things better with Margaret:

1) Phone her, say he didn't mean for the toast to hit her, but then complain that his toast was burnt and that she cooked his eggs too long.

2) Do and say nothing in the hope that Margaret will forget about the errant piece of toast.

3) Phone Margaret and offer a heartfelt apology.

4) Go home immediately, apologize and say he will give up his golf game that evening and take Margaret out to supper.

Margaret, no doubt, can forgive George in any of the above scenarios. Her forgiveness does not hang on what George decides to do. Nevertheless, the fourth course of action goes a lot further towards healing the bruised relationship than do the first two. Here, George actually makes a sacrifice as a way to restore the lost harmony.

It helps to keep a human example like this in mind as we begin to consider why God should forgive our sins. God does not need to be bought off with some sacrifice; he can forgive us no matter how self-centred or unrepentant we are. But God has chosen that his forgiveness be offered in response to the perfect human effort to seek that forgiveness.

Jesus did not come to earth to be killed. He was not on a suicide mission from God. He came to form a people into a community which wholly embraced the love of both God and neighbour. Yet he knew his crucifixion was the utterly predictable result of living out his mission faithfully.

It was Jesus' faithfulness through suffering to the point of death which the Father received as an offering of reconciliation on behalf of humanity. The offering was a suitable atonement for the sins of humanity, first, because Jesus was sinless himself and had no need to seek forgiveness and, secondly, because Jesus explicitly made his offering on behalf of humanity.

The *Catechism of the Catholic Church* states this succinctly: "This sacrifice of Christ is unique; it completes and surpasses all other sacrifices. First, it is a gift from God the Father himself, for the Father handed his Son over to sinners in order to reconcile us with himself.

"At the same time it is the offering of the Son of God made man, who in freedom and love offered his life to his Father through the Holy Spirit in reparation for our disobedience" (no. 614).

We ourselves have the possibility of salvation because the day before he died, Jesus made his offering available to us through the Eucharist. Jesus established a priesthood which would be able to recreate his offering of his body and blood for those in his new community after he left our midst.

Jesus didn't throw toast or commit any other sin and his sacrifice was something far, far greater than giving up a game of golf.

Reflecting on Christ's passion and death can teach us a lot about God's love for humanity as well as about how we ought to live as followers of Jesus.

It shows us the abominable effects of sin — that God must allow himself to be killed in order that our sins might be atoned for. Our striving to avoid sin will not retroactively erase the crucifixion, but it will lessen our role in making it necessary.

The crucifixion also shows the enormity of God's love for us. "For God so loved the world that he gave his only Son, so that everyone who believes in him may not perish but have eternal life" (John 3:16). We can share in God's love by participation in the sacraments and by performing actions which take that love out into the world.

Further, like Jesus, we need not always insist on our fair share of the world's goods. We can imitate the humility, perseverance and obedience of Christ by accepting injustice done to oneself.

But we can also know that, through Christ, God shared in every form of human suffering. He is in solidarity with us in our darkest moments and we can strive to be in solidarity with others in their times of desolation.

26

The Absence of God

Read: *Catechism of the Catholic Church*, nos. 624-637

One evening last summer, our family went to the neighbourhood playground. Totally rebuilt two years earlier with lots of slides, tunnels and other apparatus for the modern child, the playground is a major source of delight for our two young girls.

Prior to this visit, however, vandals had built a fire underneath one of the plastic tunnels used by toddlers, burning a large hole in it. Children could no longer crawl through this tunnel.

Natasha, 3, was startled by this happening. "Why?" was her repeated question regarding the destruction of the tunnel. Her parents were unable to provide a satisfactory answer. Not that any answer would do. "Why? Why?" continued her shocked and puzzled refrain.

Natasha was not much interested in the playground that evening. She avoided the other apparatus and was soon ready to leave. On the way home, she clung close to her mother and the happy, carefree air of our walk to the playground was gone. It was as though her youthful innocence had been confronted by what Cardinal Joseph Ratzinger calls "the exposed nature of existence."

Ratzinger once wrote a few pages about one of the neglected truths of our faith — Christ's descent into the dead (*Introduction to Christianity,* pp. 223-30). There, he declared that "not only God's speech but also his silence is part of Christian revelation."

The experience of God's silence, or his absence, is one of the most unsettling human experiences. We are taught that the loving God is everywhere and in all things. There is enormous comfort in that and it can help us to endure great suffering.

Yet, there can come times when nothing can keep our comfortable world rightside up. It may come in the death of a relationship, the suicide of a loved one, in the face-to-face confrontation with unspeakable evil, in the approach of one's own death or even in such lesser tragedies as having one's home broken into. One encounters not the loving care of God, but rather God's absence.

In these situations, one makes one's own Jesus' cry from the cross — "My God, my God, why have you forsaken me?" (Mark 15:34). This is a raw prayer from hell, from the absence of God.

This prayer of abandonment marks Jesus' entry into hell. Jesus, the Son of God, is one with us in our moments of utter desolation. He has been there too. And further.

The *Catechism of the Catholic Church* (no. 635) quotes the anonymous Ancient Homily for Holy Saturday: "He has gone to search for Adam, our first father, as for a lost sheep."

Think of Adam. Thousands of years in the pit. Every moment experiencing the absence of God. And then suddenly the Son of God is in the pit too. With Adam. An unfathomable love ends Adam's loneliness.

Ratzinger puts it this way: "Christ strode through the gate of our final loneliness, . . . in his passion he went down into the abyss of our abandonment. Where no voice can reach us any longer, there is he. Hell is thereby overcome, or, to be more accurate, death, which was previously hell, is hell no longer. Neither is the same any longer because there is life in the midst of death, because love dwells in it" (pp. 229-230).

One of my prayers for Natasha is that she will be preserved from the cynicism, the despair, the evil of the world. That her innocence will be preserved.

It's an impossible prayer in a world fractured by original sin. The reality of our world is that there will be times of desolation. But because Christ went into the pit, the absence of God is not the final word. Christ has broken through our abandonment and offers us his unfathomable love — the possibility of eternal life.

27

The Joy of Christ's Resurrection

Read: *Catechism of the Catholic Church*, nos. 638-658

On Easter morning, it was Mary Magdalene who was the first to discover the empty tomb. And it was to Mary Magdalene, perhaps the greatest repentant sinner in the Gospels, that the risen Christ first appeared.

Jesus found Mary outside the tomb. By then, Peter and John had gone home. But it was fitting that it was to a great sinner that Jesus should first appear. For it was she who knew sin most intimately and who thoroughly rejected sin by coming to know the mercy of Jesus. She would be the first to recognize the power of the resurrection.

Almost 2,000 years later in a Soviet labor camp, another Easter is celebrated. Father Kallistos Ware passes on an excerpt of a letter from an anonymous prisoner in that camp:

"On Easter Day all of us who were imprisoned for religious convictions were united in the one joy of Christ. We were all taken into one feeling, into one spiritual triumph, glorifying the one eternal God. There was no solemn paschal service with the ringing of church bells, no possibility in our camp to dress up for worship, to dress up for the festival, to prepare Easter dishes.

"On the contrary, there was even more work and more interference than usual. All the prisoners here for religious convictions, whatever their denomination, were surrounded by more spying, by more threats from the secret police.

"Yet Easter was there: great, holy, spiritual, unforgettable. It was blessed by the presence of our risen God among us — blessed by the Siberian stars and by our sorrows.

"How our hearts beat joyfully in communion with the great resurrection! Death is conquered, fear no more, an eternal Easter is given to us!" (cited in *The Orthodox Way*, p. 117).

We find Easter celebrated with enormous joy amidst the profound suffering and persecution of a forced labor camp. We find a great sinner

— a sheep who had been hopelessly lost but who was found by the Good Shepherd — to be the first witness of the resurrection.

The resurrection is of greatest importance to those who are stripped bare, who know they are nothing, who know that everything they have comes from Jesus. All they can do is rely on Jesus, wait for Jesus. And when the risen Lord comes it is like an earthquake which brings overpowering joy.

The result? Jesus tells Mary, "Go to my brothers and say to them, 'I am ascending to my Father and your Father, to my God and your God'" (John 20:17). It is the first time Jesus has referred to the disciples as his brothers. His death and resurrection has changed their relationship. Jesus is the Son of God and now his followers are God's adopted children.

The *Catechism of the Catholic Church* says the Father raised up the Son "and by doing so perfectly introduced his Son's humanity, including his body, into the Trinity" (no. 648). But more than this. The lives of the faithful "are swept up by Christ into the heart of divine life" (no. 655).

The resurrection does more than simply free us from sin and death. It incorporates us into the very being of God. We are invited to much more than a personal relationship with Jesus; we are invited right into God's home. The Jews awaited a political Messiah. What they got was the Son of God who enables us to share in the very life of God.

Another catechism expresses it this way: "It is the risen Jesus who gives persons of faith the ability to experience his presence. He does this by allowing them to share in his own life, by bringing them even now, in their lives here on earth, into a real participation in his new way of existence. . . . The resurrection of Christ, then, is the foundation of the Christian life of faith, prayer and spiritual growth" (*The Teaching of Christ,* fourth edition, p. 132).

Easter in the secular Western world is marked by indifference. Is this because we lack a sense of our own sinfulness, of our need for Christ's redeeming power? Is it because we are a law unto ourselves and refuse to let ourselves fall under the judgment of God's law?

There lies our unadmitted poverty. We boast of our greatness and fail to see we are nothing without God. Somehow, we need to see the resurrection through the eyes of Mary Magdalene, through the eyes of the persecuted faithful of the Soviet labor camps. Somehow we need to see the life we have been given.

28

The Ascension:
Rising to Higher Things

Read: *Catechism of the Catholic Church*, nos. 659-667

When Jesus walked on the earth, Peter walked beside him. Peter witnessed his miracles and heard Jesus preach first-hand. What better basis could there be for a strong faith, a great fidelity to Jesus, the Son of God?

Yet Peter's faith was paper thin. When Jesus said that he had to suffer and die, Peter rebuked him saying, "God forbid it, Lord! This must never happen to you" (Matthew 16:22). And when Jesus was taken prisoner, Peter denied him three times out of fear for his own safety.

But after Jesus' death, resurrection and ascension to the Father, Peter became a different man. Rather than his faith fading because Jesus was no longer around to inspire it, Peter became a dynamic leader and endured persecution and eventual martyrdom for his faith.

Why? What happened to transform Peter?

Simply put, Jesus' ascension and the descent of the Holy Spirit led the disciples to seek higher things. The ascension pointed the way — the hearts and minds of Jesus' followers must rise above the earth, rise above what is accessible to the senses.

Paul's letter to the Colossians put it succinctly: "If you have been raised with Christ, seek the things that are above, where Christ is, seated at the right hand of the Father. Set your minds on things that are above, not on things that are on earth" (3:1-2).

As long as Peter set his mind "on things that are on earth," he would have no faith. Indeed if salvation comes from what is visible, there is no need for faith. We have everything that is needed within our grasp. But the ascension calls Jesus' followers to genuine faith — "the assurance of things hoped for, the conviction of things not seen" (Hebrews 11:1).

With his passion and resurrection, Jesus ceased to perform miracles. He spent the time between his resurrection and ascension establishing his church, the means through which we receive salvation.

With his ascension, Jesus remained in bodily form, he took his human nature and integrated it into the Godhead. By doing so, he completed our redemption and gave us access to the Father. With the ascension, Jesus did not abandon us. He became present to us in new ways. He is with us when two or more gather in his name and he is physically present in the Eucharist. Moreover, Jesus intercedes on our behalf with the Father. He is a high priest "who in every respect has been tested as we are, yet without sin" (Hebrews 4:15).

We have a new way of being with Jesus. His Spirit is with us to give us faith in higher things. We are called to strip off our old selves which were rooted in earthly passions such as fornication, impurity, greed, anger, abusive language and slander. And we will be clothed with a new self full of compassion, kindness, humility, meekness, patience, forgiveness and love (see Colossians 3:5-15).

Peter wore this new self after Christ's ascension had raised his mind above the earth and the descent of the Holy Spirit gave him the power to lead this new life. It was a life which would seem utterly foolish to those whose minds were distracted by earthly things. To them, Peter would appear to be the one who was distracted and lacking in normal ambition.

But setting his mind on things that are above led him to see the cares of this world as dross. Eventually life itself meant nothing to him. If preserving his life involved compromising the things that are above, then life was an impediment to salvation. He would have to be willing to let that life go.

Tertullian, an early church father, wrote that "the blood of martyrs is the seed of Christians." This is true in that martyrdom points the way to what is most real and most important — the unseen Saviour sitting at the right hand of the Father. Our lives are so much more worthy if they too bear witness to a faith in Jesus which will not be compromised by the things of the earth.

29

The Second Coming of Christ

Read: *Catechism of the Catholic Church*, nos. 668-682

This brief section of the *Catechism* has to do with the second coming of Christ. Its existence is curious, given that the full discussion of "final things" — the last judgment, the bodily resurrection, heaven, hell and purgatory — comes later in the *Catechism* (nos. 988-1060).

Wouldn't it make more sense to include the discussion of Christ's second coming with that of the last judgment?

Perhaps. But there are three reasons for making the second coming a separate topic.

First, the *Catechism* follows the order of the Creed. The *Catechism*'s authors would naturally be loathe to skip the seventh article of the Creed — "He will come again in glory to judge the living and the dead" — and just incorporate it under the twelfth article — "I believe in life everlasting."

Second, by including this short section, the *Catechism* is able to link Christ's second coming with his resurrection and to emphasize that the second coming is of lesser importance than the salvation which has already been won for humanity through the paschal mystery. "End times" are already under way, a fact which is sometimes overlooked by those who anticipate the end of the world.

Third, this section stands out clearly as an antidote to various movements of millenarianism. Narrowly speaking, millenarianism refers to the belief that Christ and his followers will establish a 1,000-year rule before the final judgment. This view was condemned by the church in 1944. The church believes that the second coming is followed almost immediately by the establishment of Christ's eternal kingdom.

Despite the condemnation, forms of Protestant fundamentalism which are millennial in their focus are widespread and growing. The spread of movements which teach that the pope is the Antichrist and the Catholic Church the whore of Babylon is a matter of utmost pastoral concern in some parts of the world. For those who are combatting such views, the *Catechism* in this section provides a blizzard of biblical references to help in that task.

But as well as responding to this form of Protestant fundamentalism, the *Catechism* also responds to the view that the church can be exhaustively defined by its efforts at this-worldly transformation.

One task of Christ's faithful is to build right relations in this world as a sign and anticipation of the eternal kingdom. But we must be careful not be obsessively focused on this task. We live ultimately for a kingdom which is not of this world and not of human making. We do not create salvation through our good works, although our good actions can be used by Christ in the formation of his kingdom. Our job is to receive salvation, not to earn salvation through obsessive busyness.

With all these considerations in mind, it is worth scanning the points which the *Catechism* makes here about the end times:

- We are already in end times and have been since Christ's ascension (no. 670).
- The current era is "the time of the Spirit and of witness." Evil and suffering remain (no. 672).
- Jesus Christ "possesses all power in heaven and on earth" (no. 668) and he "dwells on earth in his church" (no. 669).
- The church will pass away and Christ's reign will be fulfilled when he returns to earth (no. 671).
- We don't know when the second coming will take place. It could be anytime (no. 673).
- The second coming will not occur until "all Israel" repents and recognizes Jesus as Lord (no. 674).
- Before the second coming there will be a final trial which will shake the faith of many believers (no. 675).
- Related to this time of trial is the Antichrist, a movement or person through which humanity glorifies itself in place of God (nos. 675-676).
- God's triumph over evil will be realized at the last judgment (no. 677).
- In the last judgment, there will be utter clarity about the spiritual and moral state of each person (no. 678).
- By virtue of redeeming us by the cross, Christ has the right to cast definitive judgment on each person (no. 679).

This is a brief, but fairly exhaustive, presentation of the church's view of the second coming. Built into any discussion of the final things is a call to conversion, a call to realize the crucial importance of our relationship with Christ.

One need not evoke fire and brimstone to emphasize that our choice of whether to follow Christ with our whole being will reverberate throughout eternity. Knowing the simple facts that Christ has saved us through his cross and resurrection and that he will come again in glory to establish an everlasting kingdom should, in themselves, be enough to lead us to do a searching inventory of our lives.

30

Getting to Know the Holy Spirit

Read: *Catechism of the Catholic Church*, nos. 683-701

Where Mary is, the Holy Spirit is too. Our Catholic tradition teaches that Mary leads us to her Son, to Jesus. But Mary, the Mother of God, is a human being. She has no power of her own to lead anyone to Jesus. The power working through her which has led millions of people to Jesus is that of the Holy Spirit.

And then there is Peter. The first one to declare that Jesus is the Son of the living God. The one who, out of fear, disowned Jesus, yet who, after Pentecost, led thousands of people to Christ and died a martyr's death. The one whose ministry lives on today, almost 2,000 years later, in the person of Pope John Paul II.

Yet the power in Peter's ministry which has brought millions of people to be saved through Jesus Christ comes not from him. It is the power of the Holy Spirit.

The Holy Spirit is the hidden person of the Trinity. The Spirit comes not to reveal the Spirit, but to reveal the Father and the Son. The Holy Spirit is gentle, non-assertive. Ignore the Spirit and he will withdraw. But look for the Spirit and he will come rushing in to fill you with more joy, peace, kindness and generosity than you believed were at your disposal. Open the door to the Spirit and there will be incredible manifestations of God's presence.

Mary knew about such manifestations. Filled with the Holy Spirit and pregnant with Jesus, she went to visit her cousin Elizabeth. In Mary's presence, the child in Elizabeth's womb leaped for joy. Elizabeth too was filled with the Holy Spirit.

Mary is blessed among women. She is blessed with the Holy Spirit. And this Holy Spirit is contagious. His presence is palpable. The Spirit overflows from Mary and touches those around her.

More leaping took place shortly after Pentecost. This time, it was in the presence of Peter. He and John went to the temple and saw a man lame from birth being carried in. Peter looked intently at the man and asked the man to look at him. Then Peter proclaimed, "In the name of

Jesus Christ of Nazareth, stand up and walk." The man did walk and "entered the temple with them, walking and leaping and praising God" (Acts 3:8). Again, the power of the Holy Spirit to inspire faith in Jesus.

The same sorts of manifestations occur today. In the mere presence of those with a close relationship with the Holy Spirit, people have been healed of a wide variety of maladies or have been given a deep inner peace that is not of this world.

The Holy Spirit invites us to a relationship with himself. But it is a different sort of relationship than one has with either Jesus or the Father. We know the story of Jesus' life. He took physical form as a human being and he takes physical form today in the Eucharist.

But the *Catechism* tells us "The Spirit does not speak of himself. We know him only in the movement by which he reveals the Word to us and disposes us to welcome him in faith" (no. 687).

We pray to Jesus or through Jesus to the Father. But we pray with the Holy Spirit. "To be in touch with Christ, we must first have been touched by the Holy Spirit" (no. 683). The church, in its liturgy, speaks of "the fellowship of the Holy Spirit." The Spirit prays with us and even through us. "We do not know how to pray as we ought, but that very Spirit intercedes with sighs too deep for words" (Romans 8:26).

Christians, especially myself, have too often ignored the Holy Spirit. And when we do, he withdraws and we miss out on so much of what has been made available to us. Christ died not only to free us from sin, but also that we might share in the life of the Holy Spirit. Pentecost is the fulfilment of Good Friday.

Yet rarely do we accept the life in the Spirit which we have been offered. We pray, but we do not ask the Spirit to intercede with us. We do not partake of the fellowship of the Holy Spirit and so live a truncated Christian faith.

The gentle Holy Spirit comes to us, yet if we do not welcome him, he quietly leaves. Pentecostal pastor Benny Hinn writes, "The Holy Spirit will not run away in fear, but rather he will leave your presence with a wounded heart. If he is grieved, he will gently retreat" (*Good Morning, Holy Spirit,* p. 92).

We are then left to our own devices to live the life to which God has called us. One thing is certain — we will not succeed. We will fall into various forms of impurity and coarse living. We will be without joy and our lives will bear no fruit.

Take your lead, rather, from one whose life bore abundant fruit — Mary, the Mother of God. Where Mary walked, so did the Holy Spirit. And because she welcomed the Holy Spirit, she could exclaim, "My soul magnifies the Lord, and my spirit rejoices in God my saviour" (Luke 1:47).

31

The Spirit Gives Life
to Dry Bones

Read: *Catechism of the Catholic Church*, nos. 702-747

The Holy Spirit is the hardest person of the Trinity to comprehend. The three great Western religions — Christianity, Judaism and Islam — all know the Father. They know the world could not have sprung into being and continued to exist without the action of a single Creator God.

We also have access to Jesus, the Son who is one in being with the Father. We have an historical record of his life among us, his miracles, his teaching, and his passion, death and resurrection. Concrete evidence points towards his divinity and prompts us to respond to the question — was Jesus God or was he a mad fool?

But the Holy Spirit is different. The Spirit is self-effacing. He points always to the Son and never to himself. Moreover, there is no set of facts — apart from the testimony of Scripture — which compels us to believe in the Holy Spirit or that he is God.

Indeed, the Holy Spirit was at the core of major theological controversies in the fourth century as the church struggled to write what came to be known as the Nicene Creed. Some thought the Holy Spirit was inferior to the Father and the Son. But the church eventually discerned the full divinity of the Spirit and emphasized both the uniqueness and the unity of the three persons.

Our struggle with the transparency of the Holy Spirit and with his apparent distance is a real one. And yet, paradoxically, there is no person in the Trinity who is closer to the baptized person. The Holy Spirit dwells within us and leads us to new life in Jesus Christ. It is the Holy Spirit who, through Christ's death and resurrection, restores us to the likeness of God.

Perhaps the most striking reference to the Spirit of God in the Old Testament is the account of new life being breathed into the field of dry bones in Ezekiel 37. The bones of the people are dried up, their hope completely gone. But the Lord promises, "I will put my spirit within you, and you shall live, and I will place you on your own soil" (37:14).

It is God's Spirit which gives life to the people and enables them to live up to God's law which they are so incapable of fulfilling on their own. The promise God made through the prophet Ezekiel is brought to fruition first through the return of the Jewish people from their Babylonian exile.

Later, the Holy Spirit is given much more fully to the followers of Jesus at Pentecost. The dry bones are brought to life through the covenant community we call the church.

The contrast between the field of dry bones and those people filled with God's Spirit remains pertinent in today's society. We hunger for the life of the Spirit in a world driven by materialism.

A world focused on fleeting pleasures, petty one-upmanship and an obsessive quest for a secure retirement is a world where the life of the Spirit has been truncated. It is only half human and certainly not divine.

In his 1986 encyclical, *The Lord and Giver of Life (Dominum et Vivificantem)*, Pope John Paul says that the Holy Spirit is a gift to humanity "which transforms the human world from within" (no. 59). It enables the person to rise above the material world with its "increasing signs of death."

Indeed, a materialistic orientation to living, by its very nature, points toward death. For everything material deteriorates and passes away. The Holy Spirit shows that death is not the final answer.

The Spirit reveals "the reality of the inner person, of what is deepest and most essential in the human person, because it is spiritual and incorruptible," wrote the pope (no. 58). When we, through the influence of the Holy Spirit, discover the divine dimension of life, we can be freed from materialistic modes of living.

The Spirit brings hope and a new way of life. We need not endure the futility of materialism. Nor should we seek salvation in adherence to laws. We must allow the Spirit to transform us from within. He will fulfil the Lord's promise: "A new heart I will give you, and a new spirit I will put within you; and I will remove from your body the heart of stone and give you a heart of flesh" (Ezekiel 36:26).

32

The Birthday of the Church

Read: *Catechism of the Catholic Church*, nos. 748-780

Throughout my adult life, I had celebrated Pentecost as the birthday of the church. After all, Pentecost was the day the Holy Spirit descended on the apostles and other followers of Christ. A frightened and seemingly lost group of individuals was forged into one body with a mission of bringing the good news to all nations.

That's certainly part of the story. But if we want to find the birthday of the church, we need to look for a less uplifting occasion — the crucifixion.

The *Catechism of the Catholic Church* quotes the Second Vatican Council in making the point that the church was born from the blood and water which flowed from the side of Christ as he lay dead on the cross: "'For it was from the side of Christ as he slept the sleep of death upon the cross that there came forth the "wondrous sacrament of the whole church."' As Eve was formed from the sleeping Adam's side, so the church was born from the pierced heart of Christ hanging dead on the cross" (*Catechism*, no. 766). From his death, we draw life.

Certainly this is a puzzling notion for people in the late twentiet century trained to view reality in a most literal fashion and to see the church as one more organization in society, albeit one that was divinely instituted.

However, this is one of many points where church teaching forces us to let go of our literal-mindedness and to seek spiritual understanding. Visible realities become signs of a greater reality which exists on an eternal plane.

"Mystery" is one of the most commonly-used words in the *Catechism*. In this section, it pops up several times, most notably in another quote from Vatican II: "The church 'is the reign of God already present in mystery'" (no. 763).

The church, one might say, provides a hint or anticipation of what eternal life will be. Eternal life is already a reality, but we see it, as Paul said, "in a mirror, dimly" (1 Corinthians 13:12).

Jesus' preaching of the good news then is actually the first step in the establishment of the church. The church was born on Calvary and the descent of the Holy Spirit at Pentecost sanctified the church; an everlasting seal of the Holy Spirit was put on its ministry of teaching, governing and sanctifying.

But what of this birth of the church?

On the cross, Christ fulfilled the Old Covenant and opened up to humanity the possibility of a whole new way of life. God's covenant with the Jewish people calls them to lead morally upright lives. They were called to act out of something greater than their instincts and emotions. They were called to live by a moral law which sometimes meant overcoming one's selfish desires in order to do the right thing.

But often God's people failed to live up to this moral law. They disappointed God by turning away from the law. This happened because, on their own, people do not have the ability to consistently do what is right. The inclination to sin is that overpowering.

Christ's death on the cross offered us the way to overcome sin in our lives. Christ entered into an intimate solidarity with each one of us in our pain and loneliness. And he called us to be in solidarity with him at his moment of crucifixion. We can share in the water and blood which flowed from the side of Christ.

St. John Chrysostom, the great fourth-century bishop of Constantinople, explains this further in his *Catecheses:* "Water and blood symbolized baptism and the Holy Eucharist. From these two sacraments the church is born: from baptism, the cleansing water that gives rebirth and renewal from the Holy Spirit, and from the Holy Eucharist. Since the symbols of baptism and the Eucharist flowed from his side, it was from his side that Christ fashioned the church, as he had fashioned Eve from the side of Adam."

Through baptism and the Eucharist we are fashioned into something previously unimaginable — one body in Christ, a people empowered to leave sin behind by relying on God's presence in the graces of the sacraments.

The development of a people united with God through Christ's death on the cross is a great mystery, one which stretches human understanding. This mysterious body is something quite different than what sociologists can analyze. Yet, it is something which we continue to live today, united through the water and blood from Christ's side with all other Christians over the last 2,000 years and into an undetermined future.

33

We Are Christ's Church

Read: *Catechism of the Catholic Church*, nos. 781-810

In our Edmonton Archdiocese, we recently went through a synod process, a process aimed at renewing the life of the local church. Sometimes in our discussions, we started sentences with the words, "The church should . . .".

It's a revealing phrase. Revealing because it can set up the church as separate from those of us having the discussion. It's not always clear what or who this church is. Is it the bishops and priests? Is it the staff at the pastoral centre? Is it Vatican bureaucracy?

One thing, however, is clearly implied: We are not the church; the church is someone or something else.

The *Catechism*, following in the steps of the Second Vatican Council, should force us to re-examine how we talk about the church. It describes the church by using three images: the people of God, the body of Christ and the temple of the Holy Spirit.

At its heart, the church is less an institution than it is a communion of love among the baptized and between the baptized and God. "The church's first purpose is to be the sacrament of inner union of humanity with God" (no. 775).

Nor is the church a community the way a neighbourhood league, the Rotary or even your local parish are communities. It is not a collection of people who have come together on their own volition for some common purpose.

To be sure, the church is a people. But it is not a people who have a lock on God. Rather, it is a people God acquired for himself "from those who previously were not a people" (no. 782). God is the one who takes the initiative, not us.

This people of God has a structure of authority. The head of the church is Jesus Christ. The rest of us, however, are not his slaves. We are his body. We share in his priestly, prophetic and kingly ministry. Just as "Christ is the light of all nations" (Vatican II, *Constitution on the*

Church, no. 1), so are we. We each have a vocation to be holy as Christ was holy.

The church is not a democracy. Nor is it a dictatorship. The church is the sacrament of salvation. As such, people perform different roles of service within the body. Unity within the body does not destroy the diversity among God's people. The body cannot be identified with just one of its parts (1 Corinthians 12:14).

That is the error we make when we speak as though the church were the pope, his staff and the bishops. The church has a hierarchy, but the hierarchy is not, by itself, the church. Nor are we the vassals of the hierarchy. All have equal dignity before God; all share equally in Christ's saving mission. All have equal responsibility for carrying out that mission.

Our secularized society treats the church solely as a social organization. And not a particularly attractive organization at that. But we insist that it is more, much more. We insist on the transcendence of God and on the transcendent nature of Christ's church.

A society which turns its back on God will not sense the mystical unity of being and, in particular, the mystical unity of God's holy people. It will see only individuals and gatherings of individuals.

This secularist viewpoint sees the individual as either a decision-maker or the object of someone else's decision-making. It assumes that the dignity of the person is rooted in being an autonomous self-determining subject.

Christians insist that human dignity is God's gift. We say that dignity stems from God creating us in his image and likeness and that our fulfilment comes when we are united with God. The church is the foretaste of such union.

As such, we see the greatest witness to human dignity lying not in the radical assertion of one's uniqueness, but in answering God's call by saying, "Let it be with me according to your word" (Luke 1:38). The greatest thing a person can be is not famous, flamboyant or rich, but the handmaid of the Lord.

Herein lies the source of the *Catechism's* statement that "the 'Marian' dimension of the church precedes the 'Petrine'" (no. 773). Peter was the first pope, the first vicar of Christ. But Mary is the one all Christians should imitate. And the church is most perfectly embodied by Mary, not Peter.

Mary, as we shall see, is the mother of the church. A church which ought to be understood as the people of God, the body of Christ and the temple of the Holy Spirit.

34

The Oneness of the Church

Read: *Catechism of the Catholic Church*, nos. 811-822

One of the most exhilarating experiences of my life was attending the 1983 World Council of Churches assembly in Vancouver. The event was a three-week reflection on Jesus Christ: The Life of the World. It brought together leading theologians and church leaders representing a dazzling array of Christian denominations from around the world.

I realized the event was going to be special the day before it began when Archbishop Robert Runcie of Canterbury, head of the world Anglican Church, got in the lineup behind me to get his delegate credentials. After our brief chat, he was whisked up to the front of the line. (Imagine the pope having to line up to get his delegate's badge!)

The assembly was an all-too-brief immersion in the music, liturgy and prayer of Christians ranging from Russian Orthodox to African Methodists. (Roman Catholic participation was minimal.) My heart soared as I sang Taizé chants with Brother Roger, founder of that remarkable French community, and listened to a passionate midnight talk by South African Bishop Desmond Tutu.

The impression of the enormous diversity of the church made during those three weeks left an indelible mark on me. At first, it was difficult to return to parish worship. The sameness of the liturgy from week to week and the half-hearted participation of the congregation paled next to what I had encountered in Vancouver.

But a deeper problem with which I struggled for many years afterwards was that of the oneness of the church. Jesus Christ had founded one church, one body. Yet, my most profound experience of the WCC assembly was of the church's diversity. What, however, was the source of the church's unity?

This was not just an intellectual question. It was something I mainly experienced on a gut level. In fact, at the time, I don't think I could have described this struggle in words. My commitment to the Roman Catholic Church eventually turned lukewarm. I sometimes worshipped at other Christian churches, not so much out of an ecumenical commitment as out of spiritual drift. I once made a Mennonite congregation my home for a few months. But really I was homeless, a spiritual nomad.

Emotionally, I returned home that day in 1989 when, having moved back to Edmonton after four years in Winnipeg, I first stepped into St. Joseph's Basilica. I experienced a warm embrace from the people, from the very building itself.

Intellectually, I returned home by gaining new eyes for the teachings of the Second Vatican Council. Sometimes Vatican II is presented as a break with the past. But what I now see in those documents is a respect both for other Christians and for the Roman Catholic heritage. Other Christians are seen as gifted by the Holy Spirit, rather than as lost souls on the road to perdition. But the council also held firm to the teaching that the Catholic Church is the church founded by Christ.

All of this is wrapped up in the council's statement that "The church, constituted and organized in the world as a society, subsists in the Catholic Church, which is governed by the successor of Peter and by the bishops in union with that successor, although many elements of sanctification and of truth can be found outside of her visible structure" (*Constitution on the Church*, 8).

During the 1960s when those words were written, most of the attention was focused on the last part of the sentence. It was novel for Catholics to say sanctification and truth can be found outside of full union with Rome. Indeed, that was surely my own experience at the Vancouver assembly. Truth and sanctification abounded there.

Yet, some things were missing. The assembly spent three weeks discussing Jesus Christ: The Life of the World, much of it focused on social justice issues of life and death such as nuclear weapons and Third World oppression. But there was nary a mention of other threats to life such as abortion, contraception and euthanasia. One would have to turn to Pope John Paul to receive the fullness of *The Gospel of Life*.

So we also need to focus on the first part of that statement from the *Constitution on the Church*. We don't need to wait for visible unity among all Christian churches to experience the oneness of the church. It already "subsists" in the Roman Catholic Church.

As Pope John Paul stated in his 1995 encyclical *That All May Be One,* "God has *already* manifested the church in her eschatological reality. . . . The elements of this already-given church exist, found in their fullness in the Catholic Church and, without this fullness, in the other communities" (14).

The truth and sanctification I found in other Christian churches "derives from the fullness of grace and truth that Christ has entrusted to the Catholic Church" (*Catechism*, 819).

The Reformation was a tragic time in church history, a time which has left the church with a heritage of sinful division. But we ought not to believe that all sins lay on the side of the reformers. Far from it. In many ways, the reformers were calling the church to express some elements of the Gospel more fully. No doubt there were problems with how they expressed the call of the Spirit. But, just as surely, the Catholic response was defensive and overly eager to excommunicate.

So we struggle in the midst of the pain and the richness of Christian diversity. We seek to be one as Jesus and the Father are one (John 17:22). And we await that glorious liturgy at the end of time when all God's people bring together diverse voices of varied times and cultures to praise God fully united in one heart.

35

The Holiness of the Church

Read: *Catechism of the Catholic Church,* nos. 823-829

When we describe the church as holy, we confront the paradoxical nature of the church. Just as in the last chapter when we spoke of the church as one, it doesn't seem to gibe.

To say the church is holy in the face of the Inquisition, the Crusades, the conquest of the Americas and today's sexual abuse scandals seems to severely distort reality. The church is not holy or divine in nature, one might argue; it is human, all too human. It is the work of men and women — mostly men — and not the work of God.

Indeed, throughout the centuries, several movements have sought to drive the sinfulness out of the church. Movements such as the Donatists, Waldenses and Jansenists have, at various times and in various ways, tried to preserve the purity of the church through revulsion against priests, bishops and popes who were public sinners. Some of these purists were burned at the stake — an act which only seems to support their point.

The church, on its better days, has responded by maintaining that the sacredness of the sacraments does not depend on the sinlessness of the priest administering them. It has also responded in the light of Christ's parable of the weeds of sin mixed with the good wheat (Matthew 13:24-30). Leave the weeds alone, said Jesus, "for in gathering the weeds you would uproot the wheat along with them."

The church sanctifies the world not in spite of the sinfulness of its makers, but right in the midst of sin. Our work is to be like Christ whom God made "to be sin who knew no sin, so that in him we might become the righteousness of God" (2 Corinthians 5:21). The duty of the church is not to separate itself, but to exist in the midst of the muck of sin.

Through the church, the holiness of God becomes apparent, not the holiness of men and women. Christ, executed like a sinner, is in complete solidarity with us in our sinfulness. The church is the vehicle for God's holiness and God's mercy to be made known to the world even, paradoxically, through people who are themselves profane.

We cannot separate Christ from his church. We cannot conclude that the church is a degenerate "institution" as distinguished from Christ who is the Holy One.

Such a dualism would ultimately be a counsel of despair. For if there is no vehicle in this world to inaugurate us into the life of Christ, then there is no hope of salvation. If we must rely on our own holiness or on the holiness of others, we are doomed. We are all great sinners.

Hope can be found through the church precisely because it is holy. "United with Christ, the church is sanctified by him through him and with him she becomes sanctifying," says the *Catechism of the Catholic Church* (no. 827).

The *Catechism* further emphasizes this point with a quote from Pope Paul VI's *Credo of the People of God:* "The church is therefore holy, though having sinners in her midst because she herself has no other life but the life of grace. If they live her life, her members are sanctified; if they move away from her life, they fall into sins and disorders that prevent the radiation of her sanctity" (no. 827).

We don't make the church; it is a gift we receive. It is not the result of our own initiative or activity, but rather is something which is done "with me according to your word" (Luke 1:38). Our role is to cooperate with the holiness of God and to pass on the gift of life which he offers us. We become holy to the extent we cooperate with God.

In the first chapter of his letter to the Galatians, Paul tells the story of his conversion and ministry. One might think he was boasting of his exploits. But read to the end of the story and find out that it was not Paul doing these things. Paul is dead. "I have been crucified with Christ; and it is no longer I who live, but it is Christ who lives in me" (Galatians 2:19-20).

The possibility of life is open to us too. We gain it not through our own merit or activity, but through an acceptance of the love Christ makes available to us through the holiness of the church.

36

The Church Is Catholic

Read: *Catechism of the Catholic Church*, nos. 830-856

In their inspiring book, *Rome Sweet Home*, Scott and Kimberly Hahn tell of their conversions to the Catholic Church from Presbyterianism. Scott was the first to draw close to the church and he wasn't receiving much encouragement at home. So he sought out priests for advice and information.

"I asked one of them, 'Father Jim, how would I go about converting to the Catholic Church?'

"'First,' he said, 'please don't call me "Father." Second, I don't think you really need to convert! The best thing for you to do is simply to be the best Presbyterian you can be. You'll do more for the Catholic Church if you just stay put'" (p. 66).

Scott was astonished by this attitude which he says he encountered on more than one occasion. Here he was feeling called in the direction of the Catholic Church and yet the church didn't seem to want him.

That attitude of icy indifference to potential converts has probably changed somewhat in the decade or more since Scott Hahn began his approach to the church. The Rite of Christian Initiation of Adults has become well-established and is even seen as a necessary part of parish life. Few parishes or priests would turn their backs on potential converts who come knocking on their doors.

But it's still important to examine the attitudes which underlay Father Jim's rebuke to Hahn. Father Jim may call his attitude an ecumenical one. But it is surely not that. It is an attitude, rather, of indifference. This indifference does not necessarily involve respect for those with divergent understandings. It rather shows a lack of respect for religious truth and for each person's struggle to find that truth.

A genuine ecumenism would certainly not try to steal the faithful from other Christian denominations. But it would be ready for real dialogue, a respectful engagement between two parties with different understandings of the mystery of Jesus Christ, God made human.

For Catholics, a discussion of the four marks of the church — that it is one, holy, catholic and apostolic — is an essential part of that discussion. The previous two chapters looked at the Catholic Church's claim to be one and holy. More pertinent to the rebukes Hahn received, however, is the church's claim to be catholic.

The *Catechism* teaches that there is a double sense in the meaning of the word "catholic." There is a sense in which a catholic church has "a mission to the whole of the human race" (no. 831).

A catholic church is not a national church, it is a church with a mission to all nations. It is missionary in the sense that it endeavours to unite all people, even all creation, in Christ.

But there is also the sense — which is mentioned much less — which says a catholic church is one which has received from Christ "the fullness of the means of salvation." In other words, a church which is truly catholic does not rely solely on Scripture or baptism, but on "correct and complete confession of faith, full sacramental life and ordained ministry in apostolic succession" (no. 830).

Moreover, the *Catechism* treats this second meaning as more fundamental. To the extent that the church has a mission to the whole world, it must first possess the fullness of the means of salvation. And further, we recognize the true church more by its possession of this fullness than by its being spread around the globe.

If we believe the Catholic Church possesses the fullness of the means of salvation, then we must conclude Father Jim was doing Scott Hahn a grave disservice. He was steering him away from the fullness of the faith.

In a similar manner, we can cheat ourselves if we accept only part of what the church teaches or only some of the graces which it offers. The Second Vatican Council introduced the notion of a hierarchy of truths to express the notion that some truths of the faith — such as the Trinity and the divinity of Jesus — are more central than others (see *Catechism*, nos. 90, 234).

But this notion does not mean we should accept only the most important truths and neglect the others. For our faith to be full and to bear fruit, we should believe all that the church teaches. Our concern should be with knowing the fullness of the truth, not with adhering to as little as one can get away with while still remaining Catholic.

In fact, being catholic means buying the whole meal, not just enjoying a smorgasbord where you choose what you like and leave the rest. It is God, not human beings, who has cooked the meal. If we are serious about overcoming self and following Christ, then we will surely accept that catholic faith in all its fullness.

37

A Church Founded
on the Apostles

Read: *Catechism of the Catholic Church,* nos. 857-870

One feature of modern times in the Western world is the dazzling array of churches. At the end of the first millennium, there was one united Christian church, with only a couple of separated offshoots; at the end of the second millennium, there are thousands of independent churches.

Yet Christ taught that we are one body. And he promised the apostles to be "with you always, to the end of the age" (Matthew 28:20). In the midst of all these churches with contradictory beliefs and interpretations, where is Jesus Christ? Who speaks for him today? How do we know who is speaking the truth and who is providing human interpretations and opinions?

Part of sorting out this issue involves asking who today has the faith of the apostles? Early in his public ministry, Jesus chose twelve "to be with him, and to be sent out to proclaim the message" (Mark 3:14). The apostles were not just ordinary followers of Jesus; Jesus identified himself with them. "Whoever welcomes you, welcomes me," he told them (Matthew 10:40).

At the Last Supper, Jesus made a crucial promise to the Twelve which he did not extend to his other followers: "When the Spirit of truth comes, he will guide you into all the truth" (John 16:13). Thus, while Jesus revealed truth to many people, only the apostles were given a special guarantee of knowing the truth. The Twelve — whose names all four Gospels took care to list — had a charism for keeping the truth intact and revealing it to all humanity.

Christian churches all generally accept the importance of the apostles. Where they begin to differ is on whether the mission of the apostles could be passed on to others as the original Twelve died. In the early Christian community, there was widespread belief that Christ's second coming would take place before the last apostle died.

Many Christian churches believe that the mission of the apostles could not be passed on, that it was unique. They see the apostolic faith being preserved and renewed only through the seemingly random outpouring of charismatic gifts by the Holy Spirit. From this point of view, the presence of signs and wonders guarantees God's presence in the church.

In one sense, it is true that the apostles' ministry was unique. They were eyewitnesses to Christ's public ministry and to his resurrection. When they died, there could be no new Christian revelation.

But in the Scriptures, we see the apostles attempting to pass on the ministry of preserving the truth which was entrusted to them. Of particular interest are the efforts of Paul — who had been accepted as an apostle — to pass on his ministry to Timothy. Indeed, his second letter to Timothy makes little sense except in the context of the passing on of ordained ministry.

Timothy, the first bishop of Ephesus, had received "the gift of God" through the laying-on of hands (2 Timothy 1:6; 1 Timothy 4:14). And he is urged to "Guard the good treasure entrusted to you, with the help of the Holy Spirit living in us" (2 Timothy 1:14). Both Timothy and Titus, though never called apostles, received a mandate to teach, govern, and ordain deacons, priests and bishops.

Thus, although the church is "built upon the foundations of the apostles and prophets" (Ephesians 2:20), their mandate endures even after they are gone. This is the fulfilment of Christ's promise to be "with you always."

It is also important that there be historic continuity of today's ordained ministers with the apostles themselves. The apostolic ministry cannot be entrusted to a person by others who have not also received that ministry. If the line of succession is broken, those who come after are not true spiritual successors of the apostles.

Understood in this way, only the Roman Catholic and Orthodox churches are true inheritors of the apostolic tradition. This does not mean Christ is not present in other denominations. Those churches can be places for great outpourings of God's grace. Their members can be baptized, pray and read Scripture.

All this is of great importance. But it does mean that those churches have lost most of the sacraments and have lost the guarantee that they are passing on the teachings of the apostles. And when they confront new questions, not directly dealt with by the apostles, there is no assurance that their answers are the ones that would have been given by Christ and the apostles.

Fidelity to the apostolic tradition is not without consequences for the life of the Catholic and Orthodox churches. This fidelity dictates a hierarchical structure of church and it also gives those churches a special responsibility to work for Christian unity.

Further, rather than being a reason for Catholics and Orthodox to boast, it imposes a duty to submit ourselves to the teaching and authority of the successors of the apostles. We must learn our faith, believe it with great fervour and pass it on to others. Frequently, we must ask ourselves how well we are fulfilling that responsibility.

38

"Domination"
by Church Hierarchy

Read: *Catechism of the Catholic Church*, nos. 871-896

In the eyes of many today, the existence of a hierarchy in the Catholic Church is a counter-witness to the Gospel. It shows that the church is just like any other social organization with a few bosses and lots of minions. Power lies in the hands of those at the top while those at the bottom of the pyramid are marginalized.

The church talks about the equality of the baptized. But really there is no equality. The church is just another institution of domination.

Or so the argument goes.

It must be said that the Catholic Church is among the most hierarchical of all established religions. But such hierarchy exists not for the development and hoarding of worldly power. Rather, it is the means through which Christ continues to act in the world today.

To be sure, ordination has sometimes carried with it worldly power and wealth. The priesthood has sometimes been seen as a way out of poverty and into a good education, rather than as a way of becoming one with the poor. And the priesthood and religious life have been stained by the revelations of sexual abuse in numerous locales across the Western world in the last decade. Such stains are not new — church history is rife with examples of faith being polluted by power.

The use of the priesthood for the pursuit and exercise of power, however, must be seen as an abuse. The hierarchy exists to serve the people of God and to build up the body of Christ, not to ride roughshod over the faithful. Throughout the church's history, reform movements have continually sprung up to renew the priesthood and religious life whenever the Gospel was too widely compromised.

Jesus told his followers to "call no one on earth your father" (Matthew 23:9). This remains essential advice. We must put no person above God. We are all here to serve God. And the pope carries the largest burden of service.

No one can ordain himself a priest. No one, no matter how inspired by God, can erect their own Catholic church, hang out a shingle announcing Mass times and start their own church community. The priest does not receive ordination on his own authority. He is called to act in the person of Christ and receives his ordination from a bishop who has himself received the fullness of the priesthood.

Christ promised to remain with us "to the end of the age" (Matthew 28:20) and the sacraments of the church are a primary way that he is present to us. So the dispensing of God's gifts to all members of the body takes place through some members especially authorized to act in the person of Christ. Moreover, not anyone can authorize a person to become a priest. For someone to be properly authorized to act in the person of Christ, he must receive that office from someone else in a direct line of succession from the apostles.

The office into which one is ordained is that of teaching, governing and sanctifying God's people. The priest does not teach his own opinions; nor should he make up rules to suit his own desires; he does not dispense his own gifts like some ecclesial Santa Claus. Again, he acts in the person of Christ.

The main ministry is that of sanctifying God's people — leading them to holiness. The ministries of teaching and ruling exist for higher end of sanctifying. Being ordained does not necessarily make the priest holier than the laity. But it does give him the ability and responsibility to lead people closer to God.

One adult catechism puts this succinctly: "the essential activity of the church is its spiritual life: its believing, hoping and loving, and its services of teaching and shepherding that nourish such life in Christ. All the external structures and activities of the church exist to serve the spiritual purposes" (*The Teaching of Christ,* fourth edition, pp. 158-59).

The *Catechism of the Catholic Church* strongly emphasizes the dimension of priestly service: "Entirely dependent on Christ who gives mission and authority, ministers are truly 'slaves of Christ,' in the image of him who freely took 'the form of a slave' for us" (no. 876). The minister is called to lose himself so Christ can teach, govern and sanctify.

The hierarchy thus exists to be a ministry of service, not power. "Whoever wishes to be greatest among you must be your servant," Jesus told the Twelve (Matthew 20:26).

Indeed, our church is now striving to replace symbols of power with those of service. Gone is the papal tiara with which popes had been crowned since the Middle Ages. Gone too are the footmen who used to carry the pope on his throne around St. Peter's Square. For the hierarchy exists not to dominate, but to serve.

39

The Laity:
Renewing the Secular World

Read: *Catechism of the Catholic Church*, nos. 897-913

Question #4 of the old *Baltimore Catechism* asks, "What must we do to gain the happiness of heaven?" The succinct answer: "To gain the happiness of heaven we must know, love and serve God in this world."

The *Baltimore Catechism* might have added that this answer applies to lay people as well as to priests and religious. While that might seem like belabouring the obvious, it is far from obvious to many today.

Peter Kreeft, a philosopher at Boston College, a Catholic university, routinely asks his students why God should allow them into heaven after they die. Well over three-quarters of them don't know. "Their answer to that question is something like 'be sincere' or 'try your best' or 'don't hurt people' or 'work for peace' or some such trumpet blast" (*Fundamentals of the Faith*, p. 15).

Such ignorance displays not only a lack of knowledge about the Catholic faith, but also betrays an assumption deeply ingrained in the Catholic psyche — that the life of faith is something for priests and religious and is not something with which lay people need to be bothered.

This assumption has been a disaster for both church and society as well as lay people themselves. It leads to minimal religious participation by even so-called active Catholics and to a legalistic morality with many "don'ts" and few "do's." It discourages evangelization and leaves secular society without the influence of Catholic values. Our society is in a state of decay, even collapse, in no small part because faith and life are treated as separate entities with no effect on each other.

This problem is the flip side of the issue I examined in the previous chapter on the church's hierarchy. If the hierarchy is identified with power in the church, laity must be identified with lack of power or responsibility. With encouragement from Second Vatican Council documents, people have tried to redress this perceived power issue by allowing laity to perform some roles previously reserved for clerics.

While such involvement has merit, a sole emphasis on this approach tends to solidify the assumption that the real work of the church is that traditionally done by priests. This assumption, quite simply, is a new form of clericalism. The church needs to shake it out of its system as rapidly and as thoroughly as possible.

The main thrust of Vatican II teaching on the laity is, in fact, quite different. The council said laity are called to "work for the sanctification of the world from within" (*Constitution on the Church,* 31). Again, their job is that of "fashioning and perfecting the sphere of earthly things according to the spirit of Christ" (*Decree on the Laity,* 4). And the goal of the laity is nothing less than "the renewal of the whole temporal order" (no. 5).

This is a mighty task and also one of great dignity. It involves not a power struggle with the clergy, but a working-together towards a common end by serving in complementary ways. The formation of laity for this task will be as extensive as the formation of priests. And such formation will continue throughout life as we seek greater maturity in the faith. It will not only impart knowledge, but also develop holiness.

Formation programs in the church reveal where the church is putting its energy. Russell Shaw, director of public information for the Knights of Columbus, observes that "although many programs of education and formation are now available to laymen preparing for ministry, systematic formation of the laity to undertake their secular duties in the spirit of apostolate is almost totally lacking" (*To Hunt, To Shoot, To Entertain: Clericalism and Catholic Laity,* p. 94).

Pope John Paul, in his 1988 statement on the laity, outlined such a program of lay formation in terms of spiritual formation, formation in doctrine including church social teaching, and the cultivation of human values (*Christifideles Laici,* 60).

The church's social doctrine is sometimes described as its best-kept secret. But really social teaching is probably no less understood than are numerous other aspects of church teaching. Moreover, it cannot properly be understood except in the context of the full range of doctrine. Church social teaching will find its feet once laity *en masse* find their vocation of service within the body of Christ.

That body is not to be restricted to liturgical celebrations in church buildings. It ought to walk out of the sanctuary into the streets and institutions of the secular world. Nothing is exempt from the healing touch of Christ's hand. And it is the unique service of lay people to be that hand which reaches out and touches the world in places where it is hurting the most.

40

Consecrated Life:
Visions for Transformation

Read: *Catechism of the Catholic Church*, nos. 914-945

The various forms of consecrated life fulfil many roles in the Catholic Church, one of which is to serve as a weather vane. When new religious orders blossom in the church it is invariably in response to needs which are not being met.

New religious orders, by their very existence, often point to weaknesses in the church or society. Because of that, if we want to improve the life of the church, it is important to pay close attention to how these new orders perceive their mission.

Why is this so? Consecrated life is, in fact, a way of living out one's baptismal commitment with great fervour, making one's life "dedicated totally to God" (*Catechism of the Catholic Church*, no. 916). Of course, all the baptized should be totally dedicated to God. What is unique about those in consecrated life is that they express their dedication through vowed lives of poverty, chastity and obedience.

Religious life finds its inspiration in the apostolic community described in the Acts of the Apostles: "All who believed were together and had all things in common; they would sell their possessions and goods and distribute the proceeds to all, as any had need. Day by day, they spent much time together in the temple, they broke bread at home and ate their food with glad and generous hearts, praising God and having the goodwill of all the people" (Acts 2:44-47).

As early as the third century, Christians who were dismayed by the watered-down faith of the church began to withdraw from society to live the Gospel with greater purity. These "desert fathers" were disturbed by the ease with which Christian life could be lived following the end of the Roman persecutions and the establishment of Christianity as the state religion. They saw the Christian faith as a call, not to respectability, but to renunciation. The first monks sought to live the Gospel in a radical way.

So it has always been. St. Francis of Assisi in the thirteenth century drew followers who were upset by the worldliness and wealth of the church. In the same era, St. Dominic founded an order of preachers, men who gave up everything to study the faith and defend it from opposition. Both addressed various aspects of a church strong in worldly terms, but spiritually emaciated.

In the sixteenth century, St. Angela Merici founded an order to teach young girls with the goal of re-Christianizing family life through solid education. And in the nineteenth century, St. Eugène de Mazenod, repulsed by the identification of the church with the French aristocracy, established the Oblates of Mary Immaculate to bring the good news to the poor.

There are numerous other cases like these where men and women began institutions of consecrated life to address the perceived weaknesses of society and the church in their day. The mere existence of these vibrant organizations was a radical critique of and call to renewal for the world of that time.

As the centuries passed, those organizations have either adapted to changing times or have died. As religious orders have renewed themselves in the wake of the Second Vatican Council, we see them addressing the critical issues of the late twentieth century.

But if we want to see the spiritual crisis of our own time most clearly, we need to look at the new institutions of consecrated life which have emerged and thrived in the twentieth century. Older religious orders may well have identified some of the same issues, but it is in the new organizations that this crisis is identified most clearly.

The Legionaries of Christ, for example, were founded in 1941 by Marcial Maciel, at that time a young seminarian in Mexico. By 1991, it had over 2,000 seminarians around the world. Those seminarians spend up to 15 years in preparation before ordination — a formation which includes rigorous intellectual training, but also formation of the whole person. Spiritual formation is essential (they spend three hours in prayer a day), but not sufficient, to prepare Maciel's priests.

The legionaries are fiercely loyal to the pope and the church's magisterial teaching. But far from being a new clericalism, they see lay leadership as the hope for transforming society. They endeavour to form and work with lay people through the family, education and mass media.

But this congregation also has a strong love for the poorest and most marginalized. Its members live with the poor, especially in Latin America, and help provide basic services like clean drinking water.

Or, one might look at very different orders, the Little Brothers and Little Sisters of Jesus who live in the spirit of Charles de Foucauld. De Foucauld moved to Africa in the early twentieth century to work for the conversion of Arabs through a hidden life of prayer, penance and adoration of the Blessed Sacrament. "By taking the altar and its tabernacle into the midst of unbelieving peoples, (the Little Brothers) sanctify those peoples without saying a word, as Jesus silently sanctified the world for 30 years at Nazareth," he wrote.

Or, still further, one should note the emergence of a new form of consecrated life in the twentieth century — secular institutes whose members live in their own homes, work at everyday jobs and wear no visible sign of their consecration. Their mission is to transform the world from within, to be the yeast in the dough which causes it to rise into something new and glorious.

And if one includes still other new movements in the church — not all of which are forms of consecrated life — such as Mother Teresa's Missionaries of Charity, the Rome-based Sant Egidio community, Canada's Madonna House apostolate and Jean Vanier's L'Arche homes for the mentally handicapped, a clear picture begins to develop. One sees an emerging church which places greater emphasis on the responsibility of laity to transform society, on reaching out to the most marginalized, on adherence to the teachings of the pastors of the church, and on evangelization in complex cultures.

These qualities contain an implicit call for renewal in the life of the church. In these organizations, we can catch glimpses of the future of our church. We see a church which is faithful to its traditional teaching but which is no longer part of the establishment in society. It works quietly among small groups of people, is rooted in prayer and finds its soul among the marginalized. It is becoming more and more like the community described in the Acts of the Apostles.

41

The Communion of Saints

Read: *Catechism of the Catholic Church*, nos. 946-962

My maternal grandmother, Christina White, had a great fondness for each of her 21 grandchildren. That's a large number to get to know individually. Yet she paid great attention to our unique needs. When I was a child she made me a series of Grammie Bunnies — stuffed toy rabbits. As I wore one out from excessive cuddling, she made another.

When her grandchildren got older, she made quilts for each of us. Over the years, she made me three of them. Times 21, that's a lot of quilts.

In 1989, just five days shy of her 96th birthday, Grammie White died. Less than six weeks later, I met Nora Parker, the woman I married. Grammie always knew how to look after her grandchildren. I saw her hand in this. Nora swears she didn't act alone, that her maternal grandmother, Helen Grainger, was part of this heavenly conspiracy of grandmothers which brought us together.

Who's to know, for sure? Are we just projecting our feelings into an explanation of occurrences which are mere coincidence? Deceased grandmothers don't leave a trail of hard evidence for their actions.

Still, such intuitions about the influence of ancestors and deceased loved ones are widespread. They are not a uniquely Christian phenomenon. However, Christians do believe that each person retains their individuality after death. We do not melt into God or become an undifferentiated part of some cosmic mystical ooze.

Nor do those who die leave the church. They remain part of Christ's body, even more effective in their intercession on behalf of us and our sin-filled world than they ever could have been when they walked among us. They are close to God and, because of that, they can bring us closer to God.

The Second Vatican Council devoted significant attention to the communion of saints on earth, in heaven and in purgatory. One thing it said was that "The union of the wayfarers with the brethren who have gone to sleep in the peace of Christ is not in the least interrupted. On the

94

contrary, . . . it is strengthened through the exchange of spiritual goods" (*Constitution on the Church,* 49).

To one with an "enlightened," scientific mind, all of this is superstitious hokum. There is no scientific procedure which could show how dead people can affect the lives of the living. This doctrine of the communion of saints reveals how superstitious religion really is.

However, the belief that we should venerate the dead and that they can act on our behalf should not be casually dismissed. That so many cultures and religions include such a belief is itself evidence for its truth.

This belief can also help us move beyond the narrowness of late-twentieth-century Western society in other ways. We can cooperate with the saints by trying to do the same sorts of things in our lives that they did in theirs. One sees this particularly in religious orders which try to live out the spirit of their founder many centuries after he or she is dead. In doing so, they may well keep alive values and orientations which our society does not value. But all Christians, not just priests and religious, should have patron saints whose lives sanctify our own by their example.

Further, the notion of the communion of saints can help us see the lasting value of our own actions. Our own values and hopes can live on in the lives of those who come after us. Realizing that can make us less compulsive about the effectiveness of our own actions. The projects we begin may bear fruit long after we are gone. Our responsibility is to be faithful to our tradition and to build a solid foundation for the future.

To see ourselves as part of the communion of saints is to know our life's work is part of something much greater than its particular objectives. Each of us is part of the body of Christ, creatively collaborating with Christ and with other Christians, both living and dead, to build up God's kingdom.

Pope John Paul once described this vividly: "The eyes of faith behold a wonderful scene: that of a countless number of lay people, both women and men, busy in their daily life and activity, oftentimes far from view and quite unacclaimed by the world, unknown to the world's great personages but nonetheless looked upon in love by the Father, untiring laborers who work in the Lord's vineyard. Confident and steadfast through the power of God's grace, these are the humble yet great builders of the kingdom of God in history" (*Christifideles Laici,* 17).

42

Mary Is Our Spiritual Mother

Read: *Catechism of the Catholic Church*, nos. 963-975

Children's storyteller Laura Krauss Melmed tells of a young boy who asks his father the rather odd question: "What was the first song ever sung?" His dad replies that the first song was "a strong song, a man's song, a warrior's song, a friend's song."

Dissatisfied with that answer, the boy asks the same question of others. His little brother says the first song was "a stomping, shaking, shout song"; his sister says it was "a jumping, twirling, leap song." He asks the dog, the minnows in the brook, the birds. None of the answers will do until the boy heard the response of his mother.

"The first song ever sung was a mother's song, a hush song, a sleep song, a love song," the mother replied. And so the boy climbed into her lap and his mother sang him to sleep (*The First Song Ever Sung,* Puffin Books, 1995).

Indeed, it is a mother's song that is not only first in our experience, but also the most comforting. It is our mother who carried us inside her for nine months and who continued to be our chief comforter after birth. It is our mother who gave and nurtured life.

So it is with our spiritual life. Mary, the mother of God, transmits spiritual life to us just as our physical mothers gave us biological life. Mary's spiritual motherhood, moreover, is more than a metaphor for how she helps us grow closer to Jesus. It is real motherhood; Mary really does give life.

This is a perplexing notion, one which only makes sense if we understand the church as the body of Christ. Not as something similar to Christ's body, but as the real flesh and blood of Jesus Christ.

Pope Pius X made this explicit when he wrote: "Bearing Jesus in her womb, Mary bore there also all those whose life was included in that of the Saviour. . . . We ought to consider ourselves as having come forth from the womb of the Virgin, from which we once issued as a body attached to its head." This point has since been reiterated by other pontiffs and by the Second Vatican Council.

Mary's spiritual motherhood became a reality at the Annunciation when she willingly accepted to be not only the biological mother of Jesus, but to accept, on behalf of humanity, his redemption of us from sin. Vatican II taught that, "At the message of the angel, the Virgin Mary received the Word of God in her heart and in her body and gave Life to the world" (*Constitution on the Church,* 53).

Her acceptance reached its climax at the crucifixion when Mary stood at the foot of the cross, sharing in Christ's suffering as only a mother could. There, Jesus proclaimed her spiritual motherhood to the world "when he said to his mother, 'Woman, here is your son.' Then he said to the disciple, 'Here is your mother'" (John 19:26-27).

From that moment at which the church was born, Mary has had a special role in giving life in Christ to each of us. And each person draws nearer to Jesus by honouring and loving his mother.

Mary treats us as a mother would. She advocates on our behalf, gives us life and showers us with spiritual gifts. We should treat her with the same respect we treat our biological mother. When we neglect Mary, we are the ones cheapened by this inattention.

In the life of grace, the first song ever sung was Mary's song, a praise song, a mother's song, a love song. It was the song which Mary sang when, with Jesus growing within her, she visited her cousin Elizabeth. And, as her children, we have it as our song too. It begins, "My soul magnifies the Lord, and my spirit rejoices in God my saviour . . ." (Luke 1:46-55).

43

I Believe in the Forgiveness of Sins

Read: *Catechism of the Catholic Church,* nos. 976-987

In his immortal tale, *A Christmas Carol,* Charles Dickens describes how Scrooge was visited by the ghost of his former business partner Jacob Marley. Marley's ghost did not come unencumbered, however. A long chain around his middle was made of cash-boxes, ledgers, deeds and heavy purses made of steel.

"I wear the chain I forged in life," said the ghost. "I made it link by link, and yard by yard; I girded it on of my own free will, and of my own free will I wore it."

Like Marley's ghost, each of us has forged our own chains. Our chains may be like his or they may be made up of old videotapes, cast-iron footballs, cases of liquor, credit cards or other modern idols we adore.

Our chains would be heavy indeed if there were no way to break our shackles. Like Marley's ghost, we would be condemned to eternal enslavement unless there were the forgiveness of sins. The *Catechism of the Catholic Church* quotes St. Augustine as saying, "Were there no forgiveness of sins in the church, there would be no hope of life to come or eternal liberation" (no. 983). It's that stark.

The *Catechism* deals with forgiveness in several places, most notably in its accounts of the sacraments of baptism and penance and of the Lord's Prayer. In this brief section, it highlights the belief in forgiveness as central to Christian living.

Believing in forgiveness, of course, entails belief both in sin and in the need for those sins to be forgiven. The first of these beliefs challenges one of the key moral phenomena in the Western world at the end of the twentieth century — a sharp decline in the awareness of sin.

The social sciences have increased our awareness that one's actions can be the result of factors in one's environment, personality makeup or upbringing. That expanded awareness helps us understand the factors that may reduce one's guilt in performing acts which objectively violate moral law. One may have done the wrong thing but not be morally guilty simply because one is out of control.

However, this awareness of our conditioning has also given people a ready excuse for immoral actions. It is easier to escape personal responsibility for one's actions if one can say, for example, that they were the result of an unhappy home life.

Along with this decrease in a sense of personal responsibility for one's actions has come a decline in belief that there are moral limits to behaviour. The rise of individualism has meant that objective standards have given way to "conscience." Not the conscience of traditional morality, to be sure, but rather the view that one can arbitrarily decide, without regard to any standards, whether an action is morally justified.

When moral limits are ignored and when personal responsibility for action is explained away, there is little reason left to talk about sin. And those who are without sin don't need forgiveness.

So when we say, "I believe in the forgiveness of sins," we are going against the grain. We are saying that there is sin and that it is not a peripheral part of human living. Sin is central. And, without forgiveness, each of us would be like Marley's ghost, condemned to forever drag around the fetters of our own making.

In societies where sin is taken seriously, forgiveness can be hard to come by. Centuries-old hurts are still remembered and felt in the Balkans, Northern Ireland and other lands less technologically advanced than Canada and the U.S. People really are in chains due to a lack of forgiveness. To us, this is puzzling. "Why don't people just forgive and forget?" we ask.

While the failure to seek reconciliation is far from laudable, it does betray an awareness that sin is more than a transient occurrence, an event which can be washed away by tomorrow's rain. The failure of others to forgive may force us to ask ourselves whether we are forgiving sins or condoning them.

"Sin is before all else an offence against God" (no. 1440) and "only God forgives sins" (no. 1441). We can ask God to heal our hurts and to use us as instruments of forgiveness. But forgiveness itself is something beyond human capability.

The good news is that "Christ . . . desires that in his church the gates of forgiveness should always be open to anyone who turns away from sin" (no. 982). Sin has always been present. But Christ, through the paschal mystery, has done the impossible — he has made forgiveness accessible to all God's people.

44

The Resurrection of the Body

Read: *Catechism of the Catholic Church*, nos. 988-1004

Humanity has always wondered about so-called "last things," that is, what happens to a person after death. Various answers have been proposed — the person ceases to exist, the soul separates from the body and goes to live with God, the soul loses its identity by becoming one with God, or reincarnation.

None of these are the answer provided by Jesus Christ. Moreover, Jesus didn't just talk about what was going to happen; he rose bodily from the dead so that we too might have eternal life.

The *Catechism of the Catholic Church* notes that this is perplexing. "How can we believe that this body, so clearly mortal, could rise to everlasting life?" And it quotes St. Augustine as saying, "On no point does the Christian faith encounter more opposition than on the resurrection of the body" (no. 996).

The *Catechism* goes on to note that "The 'how' exceeds our imagination and understanding; it is accessible only to faith." We do know that it will be the same body that we have in our present existence, but that body will be transformed. "This perishable body must put on imperishability and this mortal body must put on immortality" (1 Corinthians 15:53). The body is not resuscitated, it is glorified.

St. Paul draws an analogy with planting a seed. Our earthly body is but a seed out of which will blossom our glorified body (1 Corinthians 15:36-37).

We see this in Christ's resurrection. His resurrected body was identical with his earthly body, but glorified. Although it was the same body, often he was not recognizable to those who knew him. He could pass through locked doors, but also eat a meal.

This transformation of Christ's body, incidentally, helps us understand the Eucharist. It gives us some glimmer of understanding of how Christ's body and blood can be present under the appearance of bread and wine.

This is a miracle, but it is also a sign of how totally transformed we will be in God's kingdom. Christ rose, not for his own sake, but for our sake so that we too might be born into eternal life.

Deep within this doctrine is a respect for life in this world. The person is not composed of two alien substances, body and soul, but is one being, undivided. The Greeks who believed in the immortality of the soul, but not the resurrection of the body, thus regarded the body and human history as extraneous to immortality. The soul, however, was seen as by nature indestructible.

In the Christian view, everything can be destroyed. Only God is by nature immortal. We have the possibility of eternal life, not by our own power, but by the action of God who knows us and loves us and calls us to himself. Christ is the Bridegroom, ever in pursuit of his bride. And it is God's love which makes the human person imperishable.

Cardinal Joseph Ratzinger puts it this way: "The distinguishing mark of man, seen from above, is his being addressed by God, the fact that he is God's partner in a dialogue, the being called by God. Seen from below, this means that man is the being that can think of God, the being opened on to transcendence" (*Introduction to Christianity,* p. 274).

We are called to be with God, as individuals, yes, but also as a community. On the last day, the whole human world is resurrected — our actions, our hopes, our thoughts, our relationships. We are social beings and our orientation towards God is also an orientation towards other human beings. I am immortal, but there is also a new heaven and a new earth.

This gives meaning to everything we do in this world for all of our actions will be transformed and glorified in this new heaven and new earth. It is the whole person, not just the so-called spiritual dimension, which gives glory to God. We need to nurture the seed which is our life today for how it is fed and watered now will profoundly affect how it blossoms in eternity.

Rather than losing ourselves in game shows, alcohol or the pursuit of money, we should "seek the things that are above where Christ is seated at the right hand of God. Set your hearts on heavenly things, not the things that are on earth" (Colossians 3:1-2).

This not only means that we should pray and lead devoted lives, but that the work of our hands and minds builds up God's kingdom. The whole person is called to live with God in eternity; the whole person ought to be engaged in working with God in this world.

45

Dying in Christ

Read: *Catechism of the Catholic Church*, nos. 1005-1020

Father Maximilian Kolbe lived an outstanding Christian life and died an outstanding Christian death. Shortly after his ordination in 1918, Kolbe, a Polish Franciscan, founded the Knights of the Immaculata, an organization dedicated to converting people to Christ through Mary.

A fervent soul if ever there was one, Kolbe insisted each knight be totally dedicated and live a life of personal poverty. The organization used print media extensively. By 1938, its main publication had a circulation of almost one million and there were 762 full-fledged members of the Immaculata, most of whom were specialists in some aspects of publishing.

Almost immediately after the Nazi conquest of Poland in 1939, Kolbe and the organization faced persecution. Eventually, the priest was jailed and sent to Auschwitz. There, despite torture and persecution because he was a priest, he continued his priestly work undeterred. He gave impromptu talks, heard confessions, prayed openly and counselled those who sought help.

In July 1941, a prisoner escaped and the Auschwitz authorities made all the other prisoners stand all day in the hot sun. That evening, the prisoner had not been found, so the commandant went through the crowd choosing 10 to die in his place. One man who was chosen, Francis Gajowniczek, screamed that he had a wife and children. Hearing this, Kolbe immediately stepped forward and offered to take his place, an offer that the commandant accepted.

The 10 prisoners were stripped and thrown into a starvation bunker, without food or water. Those who came by the bunker invariably heard, not moaning and weeping, but the sound of the rosary being led by Kolbe or hymns being sung to Mary. Kolbe never complained, but always prayed and encouraged the others. After two weeks, he and three others remained alive and were given lethal injections. In 1982, Kolbe was canonized as a martyr for the faith.

Kolbe's death was a most horrific one, not one many of us would choose for ourselves. Increasing numbers of people in the Western world see the best possible death as one that is quick and painless. There is growing support for legalized euthanasia from those who dread not only medical technology's ability to keep people alive, but also a slow, lingering natural death.

Yet the Christian tradition is to pray for a happy death. In the Litany of the Saints, we implore, "From a sudden and unforeseen death, deliver us, O Lord." There is no need to seek suffering — although there can be grace in the acceptance of it — but death is something for which we spend our lives preparing.

The monk, under the rule of St. Benedict, seeks "to keep death daily before one's eyes." And the medieval spiritual writer Thomas a Kempis counselled that "Every action of yours, every thought, should be those of one who expects to die before the day is out" (see *Catechism of the Catholic Church,* 1014).

Is this morbid? No, it is a recognition that we are strangers on earth; our home is in heaven. Prestige, wealth, and comfort are only of passing value. We should not neglect the legitimate concerns of life in this world. But we should judge their importance within the context of eternal life. The *Catechism* states that "Remembering our mortality helps us realize that we have only a limited time in which to bring our lives to fulfilment" (no. 1007).

Death is a natural event, but people would not die had it not been for original sin. God loved us so much that he wished to spare us death. But through our option for sin, we entered into a process of dissolution and decay. Christ, however, overcame death for us by dying himself. We can further the process of redemption by resolving to die with the same spirit that Jesus and St. Maximilian exemplified in their deaths.

In them we see the supreme virtue of love in laying down one's life for another. They showed courage in accepting an undeserved and brutal death. "Do not fear those who kill the body but cannot kill the soul" (Matthew 10:28). Both Jesus and Kolbe died with a calm resignation and forgiveness for those responsible for their deaths. And both, while not desiring to die, accepted death in obedience to the Father's will.

"It is in the face of death that the riddle of human existence becomes most acute," wrote the fathers of the Second Vatican Council (*The Church in the Modern World,* 18). No one wants to die. We all have "an eternal seed" which resists, even dreads, perpetual extinction. But that eternal seed cannot find fulfilment as long as biological life continues. We cling to earthly life and we long for something beyond it. That is the paradox of our existence.

Kolbe died a courageous death. But that death was the natural outgrowth of a life of habitual sacrifice for others, not an heroic incident tacked on at the end of an otherwise undistinguished life.

This should be an example for us. For every Christian, the process of dying with Christ to live a new life begins at baptism. "If we die in Christ's grace, physical death completes this 'dying with Christ' and so completes our incorporation into him in his redeeming act" (*Catechism*, 1010).

46

Judgment:
Facing the Truth about Our Lives

Read: *Catechism of the Catholic Church*, nos. 1021, 1038-1060

The brief story of the good thief tells of a man crucified with Jesus who saw the goodness of Jesus and the folly of his own ways (Luke 23:39-43). This good thief saw that he was getting the punishment he deserved.

Despite the mocking rebukes of the other criminal and the soldiers, and despite the lack of any evidence that Jesus would one day exercise any sort of power, this thief made the remarkable request, "Jesus, remember me when you come into your kingdom."

In response to this confession of faith and despite whatever dastardly deed this man was being executed for, Jesus responded simply, "Truly I tell you, today you will be with me in paradise."

There are many things one might ponder about this stunning incident from the life of Jesus. But one thing the church has seen in this story is a witness to a judgment each person must face at the end of life. Each person will meet Jesus to be confronted alone with the truth of their life. Those who confess faith in Jesus and sorrow for their sins will enter immediately into paradise.

Luke, however, says nothing about the fate of the criminal on the other side of Jesus.

Matthew describes a different judgment scene, in fact, a different judgment. Again, Jesus speaks: "When the Son of Man comes in his glory and all the angels with him, then he will sit on the throne of his glory. All the nations will be gathered before him . . ." (Matthew 25:31ff).

In one case, Jesus on the cross speaking to one man; in the other case, Jesus in glory faces "all the nations." Two judgments — one at the end of each person's life, the other at the end of time. Why do we need to be judged twice?

The *Catechism of the Catholic Church* describes the particular judgment each person faces at the end of life: "Each will be rewarded immediately after death in accordance with his works and faith" (no. 1021).

But this is not enough. We do not each live on an island. The effects of our actions reverberate long after our deaths. Only at the end of time will we be able to see, "even to the furthest consequences, the good each person has done or failed to do during his earthly life" (no. 1039).

So, at this last judgment, we will be judged on the opportunities to do good which we have either seized or ignored. Jesus, in this account, does not even take into account the heinous deeds we have done, only the good we have done or failed to do. Moreover, all the nations will be there to witness the truth about us, to see how we have loved or failed to love.

Many will ask why we need even one judgment. Why doesn't Jesus welcome all of us into his kingdom? All are sinners. How can God fairly decide to let some sinners "inherit the kingdom" and send others "away into eternal punishment"?

Yet the refusal to accept judgment is linked with the stubborn denial of sin. We have the possibility of sharing in divine life partly because Christ has made that possibility available to us, but also because we are free, self-determining agents of our fate. God has given us freedom to either "delight (in) the law of the Lord" or to "be driven away by the wind" (Psalm 1). The possibility of eternal life contains within it the peril of eternal punishment.

All are sinners, yet some, like the good thief, admit that the treachery of their own lives stands in sharp contrast with the unfailing goodness of God. They face the truth and are humbled by it. Others would like to be God, replacing God's laws with their own whims. Such a life is a lie.

St. John put it this way: "If we say that we have no sin, we deceive ourselves, and the truth is not in us. If we confess our sins, he who is faithful and just will forgive us our sins and cleanse us from all unrighteousness" (1 John 1:8-9).

So it was at the crucifixion. The self-righteous ones, blind to the truth, perhaps even willfully blind, mocked Jesus. But one criminal saw the profound goodness of Jesus. Because he admitted his own sin and called on Jesus to remember him, he was welcomed into Jesus' everlasting kingdom.

47

A New Heaven and a New Earth

Read: *Catechism of the Catholic Church*, nos. 1023-1029, 1042-1060

"Pie in the sky when you die." That was the taunt often hurled at Christians by Marxists and other atheists. The Christians, it was implied, only cared about the good life that would ensue after death and turned a blind eye to all suffering, even quite preventable suffering, on this side of the grave.

In one sense, this gibe was quite unfair. It was religious orders, for example, who looked after the poor and the sick and who educated the young long before worldly rulers saw it as their responsibility to attend to such matters.

But, in another sense, the gibe hit close to the mark. Traditional Catholic teaching about heaven pictured a pristine existence disconnected from life in this world. It took the Second Vatican Council to address this shortcoming. The council elaborated on the church's teaching in a way which portrayed humanity as cooperating with God in defining the shape of heaven.

The *Catechism of the Catholic Church* quotes much of the fourteenth-century definition of heaven by Pope Benedict XII. This pope's declaration *Benedictus Deus* makes up the bulk of traditional authoritative teaching on heaven. Basically, it states that, in heaven, the elect "see the divine essence with an intuitive vision, and even face to face, without the mediation of any creature" (no. 1023).

In short, in heaven we get a vision of God. We know God directly, rather than via his creation. For those who have never shown any interest in God, such a definition is unlikely to inspire them to reorient their lives. It seems to suggest that, in heaven, we are passive. For all eternity, this might seem a trifle boring.

Contemplatives could feel right at home in a heaven where all we do is "see" God. The rest of us might be highly tempted to get out and stretch our legs while we wait for something to happen.

Pope Benedict's way of phrasing this owes more to the philosophy of Plato than to Scripture. Our goal might better be described as being with God than as passively "seeing" him. In heaven, we will find the fulfilment of St. Augustine's famous cry that "our heart is restless until it rests in you." All our lives we have yearned and striven for something more than one can find in this world. In heaven, we will finally discover that "something more."

The *Catechism* refers to several Scriptural images of heaven. It is a wedding feast, the Father's house, the heavenly Jerusalem. Through these images we can understand that heaven involves a rich and intimate interpersonal sharing between God and us as well as between ourselves and other people. We sit at God's table and talk, share and celebrate with him. Heaven is a party, a home, a city. There is a buzz as well as mystical communion.

Vatican II, in a highly significant paragraph of *The Church in the Modern World* (no. 39, see *Catechism,* 1048-1050), took this further. "The expectation of a new earth must not weaken but rather stimulate our concern for cultivating this one. For here grows the body of a new human family, a body which even now is able to give some kind of fore-shadowing of the new age."

The current life is not just a testing ground to determine who wins admission to heaven. Our actions are not mere means to passing the test and getting our heavenly reward. Rather, in this life, we begin to form the next one. The steps we take now will show discernible effects in the new human family in heaven.

Each of us has hopes and dreams which are not merely self-serving. We all yearn for the eternal, that which is beyond our grasp now, that which is more than words can say. And yet that yearning is expressed in quite different ways. Some express it by working with the Third World poor, others by lives of prayer, others by knitting sweaters for their grandchildren.

What is essential is that each of us not allow that yearning to be dulled by addiction to TV, alcohol or other diversions. We need to be moved by that inner call and discipline ourselves so that it gives wing to our lives.

At the end of time, God will call together those who have been faithful to their unique personal vocations and form them into this new human family. Then we will see how the actions of each have contributed to the making of the whole.

Exactly how God will use our actions to give shape to heaven, we don't know. But Vatican II said in general what will occur: "After we have obeyed the Lord, and in his Spirit nurtured on earth the values of human dignity, brotherhood and freedom, and indeed all the good fruits of our nature and enterprise, we will find them again, but freed of stain, burnished and transfigured."

Heaven is a reward, but it is more than that. It is the fruit of our own labours in this world. It is something we have a responsibility to build. Now! The human search for heaven is not an escape from the joys and hopes, griefs and anxieties of this world. It is how we enter more fully into the human drama.

48

The Fire of Purgatory

Read: *Catechism of the Catholic Church*, nos. 1030-1032

It is only when we get close to the light that we see how stained we are.

Take St. Peter, for example. Jesus was teaching the people from Peter's boat when he asked him to go into deep water and cast out his nets. So many fish were caught that the nets began to break and the boats began to sink.

Peter saw this as a sign of Jesus' holiness. "He fell down at Jesus' knees, saying, 'Go away from me, Lord, for I am a sinful man!'" (Luke 5:8).

Peter's recognition of the holiness of Jesus drew him to an immediate awareness of his own unholiness. It took more than this momentary awareness, however, to turn Peter into a saint. Ultimately, it took fire and blood — the fire of the Holy Spirit and the blood of martyrdom. But Peter's epiphany by the lake was a key step in his spiritual growth.

It will take fire and suffering to raise us to holiness also. We can have it in this world or we can have it in the next. The great sixteenth-century mystical writer, St. John of the Cross, wrote often of the purgation of sins that we must undergo before we can be fully open to the power of God's love.

One of John's works was titled *The Living Flame of Love*. In it, he writes, "When this flame shines on the soul, since its light is excessively brilliant, it shines within the darknesses of the soul." This is what Peter experienced when he witnessed the boats overflowing with fish. The divine light of Jesus shone brightly and revealed the darkness in Peter's soul.

John went on to say, "it is impossible to perceive one's darknesses without the divine light focusing on them. Once they are driven out, a soul is illumined and, being transformed, beholds the light within itself" (1.22). For many Christians, certainly for myself, life is a matter of both running towards God and running away from his light. We love God

110

and yet his light shows us more about ourselves than we want to see. It takes great courage to let the light reveal all our hidden darknesses.

But, before the moment of death, our actions and commitments in life have revealed the direction we have chosen for our lives — to live for God or to live without him. Even if we have lived for God, however, we may not yet be able to withstand the full vision of his glory. We may need further purification; we may still need the light to reveal all our places of darkness to us.

Spiritual writers over the centuries have disagreed as to whether purgatory is a place of material punishment as well as purification. Sometimes one might gain the impression that purgatory is akin to a temporary hell.

While the *Catechism of the Catholic Church* does not exclude the possibility of material fire, it gives greater emphasis to the notion of purgatory as cleansing or purification. It states plainly that the purification experienced in purgatory "is entirely different from the punishment of the damned" (no. 1031). Purgatory does not represent condemnation; it is part of the path to holiness.

The existence of purgatory is one issue which divides Catholic and Orthodox on one side from Reformation Christians on the other. Protestants rightly look at Scripture and see great evidence for the existence of heaven and hell and virtually none for the existence of purgatory. The two main Old Testament texts used to support this belief are in books which Protestants do not accept as part of the Bible (Wisdom 3:1-9; 2 Maccabees 12:39-45).

The main New Testament evidence comes in Jesus' statement that sins against the Holy Spirit will not be forgiven "either in this age or in the age to come" (Matthew 12:32). The Catholic Church sees this as implying that some sins will be forgiven after death, yet before one gets to heaven.

Thus, while there are hints of the existence of purgatory in the Bible, there is nothing approaching proof. The real basis for our belief comes from the constant practice in the church of praying for the dead. Those in heaven don't need our prayers and our prayers for those in hell are futile. Only in some other "place" — a waiting room for heaven, as it were — could there be the dead who would benefit from such prayers.

One of the main authors of the *Catechism*, Archbishop Christoph Schonborn, writes frankly that we know purgatory exists because of the way the church prays. The church's prayers for the dead testify to the truth of the doctrine! (See *Living the Catechism of the Catholic Church*, p. 152.)

To those who believe in *sola Scriptura* — that the Bible is the sole basis for Christian doctrine — there is no solid basis for a belief in purgatory. And yet, as we have seen, sinners need purgatory. Either in this life or the next, we need to drag ourselves or be dragged into that living flame of love so that we may see the truth of our lives in the light of God's mercy and love.

49

Condemned to Hell

Read: *Catechism of the Catholic Church*, nos. 1033-1037

The Catholic Church's beliefs in hell and the devil are our most politically incorrect doctrines. Today especially, few like to hear about hell. Many see the doctrine as a harsh legacy of medieval superstition.

We find hell offensive to our understanding of God's mercy. How can anyone hold that a merciful God would condemn even unrepentant sinners to eternal punishment? Surely anyone who believes in hell must be full of resentment and a desire for revenge. And if God would condemn anyone then he must be a vengeful God.

It is a disservice to even mention hell. You'll provoke feelings of guilt and nightmares, perhaps even personality disorders.

Well, if hell is real — and Jesus taught its existence repeatedly and the church has remained constantly faithful to that teaching — then it does people no favour to silence talk about its existence. If people can go to hell, then you do them an eternal favour by telling them how to avoid the trip.

However, we know even less about hell than heaven. The *Catechism of the Catholic Church* says only that it is the "state of definitive self-exclusion from communion with God and the blessed" (no. 1033). And while the *Catechism* refers to the punishment of "eternal fire," it avoids any use of the vivid imagery of hell sometimes employed by poets, painters and preachers. It says simply that "The chief punishment of hell is eternal separation from God" (no. 1035).

But why is God so mean as to separate himself from us? The answer to this calls for a rephrasing of the question. Those condemned to hell have separated themselves from God. God does not condemn them; they have condemned themselves.

In my article on heaven, I spoke of how we build heaven in this life by cooperating with God. The damned, likewise, build their own hell through their refusal to cooperate with God.

Germain Grisez and Russell Shaw link the contemporary refusal to accept the existence of hell with a legalistic approach to morality.

People "imagine God saying, 'Here are the rules. Do as I say if you want to stay out of hell.' But God's creation is not legalistic; moral norms are moral truth. . . .

"(God) does not make arbitrary demands and run us through obedience tests. He invites us to take advantage of a wonderful opportunity, available by reason of our being created in his image and being redeemed through Jesus. To take advantage, however, we must freely do our part. And if we freely choose not to do that, not even God can do anything about it" (*Fulfillment in Christ,* pp. 220-21).

If there is both heaven and free choice, there must also be hell. There is an utmost seriousness to life. We make choices and those choices matter. They either build up God's kingdom or work against it. And in eternity, we will live out what we have made ourselves to be through these choices.

Hell is a real possibility for every person. It is the possibility that each of us have of turning our backs on God and persisting in that rejection until death.

The doctrine of hell, however, does not call us to fear and paralysis. It issues what the *Catechism* says is "an urgent call to conversion" (no. 1036). The doctrine contains a call to each person to ponder the perilous nature of our existence. Jesus advises, "Enter through the narrow gate; for the gate is wide and the road is easy that leads to destruction" (Matthew 7:13).

Jesus taught his disciples about hell not so that they could speculate about who and how many people are there and what tortures they might be undergoing. He taught this doctrine to wake us from our slumber.

To be sure, fear of hell is a less pure motive for repentance than is love for God. It is what used to be called "imperfect contrition." But a healthy dread of hellfire can start one on the way to a reformed life and the eventual love of God.

This is the sort of conversion one sometimes sees in those who have had a close brush with death. They return with a desire to do something more worthwhile with their lives than attempt to become rich or famous. A brush with death can lead one to a life of self-sacrificing love for others.

God does not want anyone to go to hell. God "is patient with you, not wanting any to perish, but all to come to repentance" (2 Peter 3:9). He does not condone sin, but he freely forgives it, if we but ask for his forgiveness and resolve to amend our lives.

Indeed God has gone as far as he could possibly go in preventing anyone from entering hell. He sent his only Son, Jesus Christ, who offered himself up for our sake so that we might have all possible means to enter God's kingdom. "God did not send the Son into the world to condemn the world, but in order that the world might be saved through him" (John 3:17).

Jesus has opened the gates of heaven. All we need to do is walk through.

50

The Case of the Missing Amen

Read: *Catechism of the Catholic Church*, nos. 1061-1065

At the end of the Apostles' and Nicene creeds comes the pithy word "Amen." Most Catholic congregations I've attended ignore this Amen. It doesn't get said.

Curious about this, I checked the Sacramentary and found that, while the Nicene Creed ends with Amen, the Apostles' Creed — the one used most frequently in Canadian churches — does not.

Puzzled, I began asking around and learned that the Amen was dropped inadvertently. The new Sacramentary, to be issued in a couple of years, will put it back in its rightful place. Whether this will in turn spur Catholic congregations to end the prayer by actually saying "Amen" remains to be seen.

Perhaps this is all a miniscule concern, a matter even smaller than the tiny word itself. Our Amen, however, says a lot. The Creed begins with the words "I believe" (or "we believe"). The Amen reiterates that "I believe" at the end of the prayer. It's like a fist to the table simultaneous with a rousing shout of "Darn right! And not only do I believe it, it's darn important too."

To say "Amen" is "to entrust oneself completely to him who is the 'Amen' of infinite love and perfect faithfulness," says the *Catechism of the Catholic Church* (no. 1064). "The Christian's everyday life will then be the 'Amen' to the 'I believe' of our baptismal profession of faith."

This ups the ante on the Amen issue a few notches. Saying "Amen" at the end of the Creed implies that by professing the Creed, I am turning my whole life over to God. I will live by the power of the invisible Holy Spirit and according to the precepts laid down by Jesus Christ. My worldly desires hold no power over me because my life is not ruled by mercurial whims of the flesh. There is something greater than me and I will bow before that "something greater" because it is sacred.

Psalm 1 points towards two ways of living. The person "whose delight is the law of the Lord" is happy. He ponders God's law night and day and ignores the advice of the wicked. Such a person "is like a tree that is planted beside the flowing waters, that yields its fruit in due season."

The wicked, however, are not planted. "They, like winnowed chaff, shall be driven away by the wind."

In today's Western world, being planted is a radical step. It says that I am not self-sufficient; I depend on the "flowing waters" for my life. To the extent that I give up my independence, I will bear fruit and my leaves will never fade.

But if I cling to my freedom, my individualism, I will be blown about like chaff in the wind. I will have my freedom but I will never bear fruit. My life will lead to doom.

By saying "Amen," I plant myself in the faith of the apostles. I proclaim that I believe all the details of the Creed including that God created earth and heaven, that Jesus, his only Son, died for our sins and rose from the dead, and that the Holy Spirit lives in the holy, catholic church.

This is belief which cannot help but shape the way one lives. It means living with one eye always turned towards eternity. It means always forgiving those who have done you wrong and always anticipating how one's thoughts and actions might affect others.

Yet, so many, especially today, live a rootless, unplanted existence. This is a false freedom which has no regard for truth. It makes self-indulgence its god. Pope John Paul notes that each person's soul has an aspect of rebellion "which leads him to reject the truth and the good in order to set himself up as an absolute principle unto himself" (*The Splendor of Truth*, 86).

True freedom, the pope says, is freedom "acquired in love, that is, the gift of self" (no. 87). Maybe we don't have the inner resources to rise from self-indulgence to love. But God will give us those resources if we rely on his power.

This does not mean turning ourselves into robots who stop thinking and feeling. It involves, as the pope says, "holding fast to the very person of Jesus, partaking of his life and his destiny, sharing in his free and loving obedience to the will of the Father" (no. 19).

Here, we can truly say "Amen." Here, we have an Amen which plants us by the flowing waters and which also gives us freedom, one rooted in love and which opens up to us the fullness of being. Amen may be a small word, but it is one which offers the possibility of a life lived with great depth.